LIKE A RIVER

CARL BRUMBACK

GOSPEL PUBLISHING HOUSE
SPRINGFIELD, MISSOURI
02-0564

LIKE A RIVER

Library of Congress Catalog Card Number 76-58782
International Standard Book Number 0-88243-564-7
Printed in the United States of America

PREFACE

"A people who have not the gratitude to record their history will not long have the virtues to make history worth recording; and no people who are indifferent to their past need hope to make their future great."[1]

Like a River is a sequel to *A Sound From Heaven*, which traced the early history of the Pentecostal Movement. The present work seeks to express the gratitude of the Assemblies of God for God's part in our history. Without Him, there would be no history; without Him, there would be no Assemblies of God.

We also seek to honor the great souls who, under God, brought this revival movement together, gave it stability, and proclaimed its message "across the nation and around the world."

A constant hope nourished by these Pentecostal pioneers was for the spread of "the fellowship of the Spirit" through the entire Church. Fearful of isolating the revival through the insulation of denominationalism, they delayed any formal organization until it became quite clear that the denominations were not going to accept the charismatic experience. Only then, and with the greatest reluctance, was the decision made to organize.

Sixty-three years later, the statistics are impressive:

The Assemblies of God has 9,140 churches, more than 20,000 credentialed ministers, over 850,000 members, and over 1.3 million adherents in the United States. Our 1,134 missionaries and 23,675 national workers serve a constituency of almost 4.6 million in 95 overseas countries.[2]

To God be the glory for this phenomenal growth! We

---

[1] Jan Gleysteen
[2] 1976 Statistics

rejoice in these numbers, not for mere numbers' sake, but for what they represent: men and women and boys and girls whose lives have been transformed by the Lord Jesus Christ, and are now reaching out to touch others.

An equal, or even greater, cause for rejoicing is the charismatic renewal that is sweeping every corner of Christendom. This mighty outpouring of the Holy Spirit is lifting the River to the floodstage! It is the fulfillment of the hope and prayer of Pentecostal believers from the first drops of this glorious Latter Rain. It is widening "the fellowship of the Spirit" to an extent unequaled since the first-century Church. Above all, it is making us very conscious of the nearness of the hour, when the Great Shepherd of the sheep will come to lead us and "other sheep . . . who are not of this fold" to that heavenly fold, where there is room for the Flock Universal!

CARL BRUMBACK

CONTENTS

CONTENTS

CHAPTER 1

"CALLING ALL SAINTS"

THE PENTECOSTAL organization known as the Assemblies of God was *Pentecostal* before it was an *organization*. This fact is vital to an adequate understanding of the Assemblies of God.

Early Pentecostalists envisioned a mighty revival sweeping the Church. It was their fervent hope and conviction that the whole Church should be Spirit-filled and supernaturally equipped to meet the twentieth-century challenge. There was no intention of establishing a Pentecostal branch of the Church, but an insistence that the entire tree was to be Pentecostal. This was the "ecumenical spirit" which pervaded the hearts of the Pentecostal pioneers—one Church—in "one accord" of Spirit fullness.

The rejection of their message by practically all of the denominations forced these idealists to face the facts of religious life. The "new wine" could not be contained in the "old wineskins." Not that it was to be necessary to give up forever their ideal of a completely Pentecostal Church ("as it was in the beginning"), but only that some objectionable elements they were to "suffer to be so *now*." Still, while reluctantly accepting the idea of a Pentecostal Movement separated outwardly from other members of the Body of Christ, no Pentecostal believer was even remotely interested in initiating a denomination which, in time, would compete with other denominations. He did not look forward to the hour when his denomination would achieve world recognition, but eagerly anticipated the hour when his own denomination would cease to exist altogether, when the Head of the Church would preside over the liquidation of all denominations and all other temporal barriers to full fellowship. Or to put it positively, he longed for "that which is perfect" to come, bringing collective as well as individual perfection—the complete and eternal unification of all believers.

He did not believe that all attempts toward unity should be abandoned until that glad hour. The prayer of Christ "that they all may be one" was to be fulfilled in "the life that now is"—"that *the world* might know." It is *here* that "all men shall know that ye are my disciples, because ye have love one to another." True "disciple love" runs through a troop of sectarianisms, and leaps over every denominational wall. It does not seek here to dissolve all organizations, as some purists propose to do, but it does constrain all to recognize a unity with all believers, regardless of organizational ties. At the same time, this love crusades according to the mind of Christ for the original purpose of the Pentecostal Revival: the outpouring of His Spirit upon all flesh, the filling of all believers with the Holy Spirit. This goal has never been, and must never be, relinquished.

* * *

The Assemblies of God cannot claim the distinction of being the oldest Pentecostal organization, but it is the *largest,* and has been since within ten years of its formation. At the beginning of the Revival, as we have seen, almost every organization was opposed to any kind of Pentecostalism and almost every Pentecostalist was opposed to any kind of organization. To see how the determined opposition to organization was broken down, we must trace the preorganizational steps.

The Apostolic Faith contingent which in 1909 rejected the leadership of Charles Parham had maintained fairly close fellowship among themselves. E. N. Bell, the Fort Worth Baptist (who had been baptized not only in water but also in the Spirit), had been selected to edit the publication *Apostolic Faith.* His able editorials, the articles sent in by other brethren, and the reports of revivals helped to bind this group together. The term "Pentecostal" gradually replaced "Apostolic Faith" as their designation, for, while they knew that the faith which they held was apostolic doctrine, they felt that "Pentecostal" did not make them appear to arrogate unto themselves apostolic office, and yet continued to identify them with the outpouring of the Spirit. It also enabled all to distinguish clearly between them and other groups which preferred the name "Apostolic Faith."

This Pentecostal group formed a strong nucleus in the Southwestern states, and not too long after breaking with Parham effected a merger with the new association of Spirit-filled believers in the Southeastern states. H. G. Rodgers was the moving force toward organization in this area. In the fall of 1909 he invited other noncommitted ministers to join him in a three-day council at Dothan, Alabama. Here they adopted the name *Church of God,* not knowing that it was already the official name of the body in Cleveland, Tennessee. H. G. Rodgers was elected moderator; Wade Ledbetter, secretary; several ministers were licensed and ordained; and steps were taken to secure recognition from the Southern Clergy Bureau.[1]

The second conference of "workers and preachers of South East Alabama and North Florida, met at Providence, Slocomb, Ala., on February 10, 1911 at 9:30 A.M."[2] About twenty preachers and a "large" number of workers were present. Seven brethren were licensed to preach, and four were ordained. Two women were given certificates as home missionaries. It was reported that four congregations had been set in order during the last year in the district, and several more were now ready. During the convention itself, forty-nine joined this *Church of God.* Rodgers wrote of those days:

Up to that time we had never been in conference and knew nothing of parliamentary law. We had no committees—no resolution committee—we did not need one. All of us were living a life of faith and preaching a gospel of love. It was inspiring to hear them

---

[1] Recognition by the various clergy bureaus was a *must* in those days of almost exclusive travel by train.
[2] Original minutes of J. W. Ledbetter, quoted by J. R. Flower, *op. cit.,* p. 18.

give their reports. They had slept on the ground and in stock barns. They had preached under trees in front yards and in brush arbors. They had lived on sardines and vienna sausages . . . had done without food for days to get a meeting started . . . but God was with us.[3]

When Rodgers and his associates discovered that they had chosen an appellation already in use, they anxiously sought a new name. Former members of the Apostolic Faith Movement had also been looking for an official title for themselves. Howard A. Goss had gone to Elder C. H. Mason, co-founder of the *Church of God in Christ,* and received permission to borrow that name. There was to be no organizational union, but the white Pentecostalists would have a name in which to issue credentials and to secure recognition from the clergy bureaus.[4]

Late in 1911,[5] or early in 1912, a merger was effected between these two groups, the newly named "Church of God in Christ" and the formerly named "Church of God." No official records are available concerning this merger, but several ordination certificates substantiate it. J. W. Welch, on June 4, 1912, and Bright Haggard, on August 20, 1912, were given credentials under the name of "The Church of God in Christ and in unity with the Apostolic Faith Movement." The January 20, 1913, issue of the *Word and Witness* invited members of both groups to attend a meeting at Dothan, Alabama, in February, 1913.

The Church of God in Christ met in Meridian, Mississippi, in June of 1913. By this time the process of merger seems to have been complete, for in a subsequent ministerial list assembled by the credentials committee of this convention, names of 352 members show leadership of both groups within the one church. Arch P. Collins of Fort Worth; E. N. Bell of Malvern, Arkansas; H. A. Goss

---

[3] *Early History of the Assemblies of God,* pp. 5, 6.
[4] This kindness by the colored Pentecostal brethren is but one example of the contribution made to the Pentecostal Movement by the colored race. The American Negro has made a permanent impression upon the Pentecostal Movement, contributing some of its outstanding personalities: W. J. Seymour, the founder of Azusa Street Mission; G. T. Haywood, composer of "Jesus, the Son of God," "I See a Crimson Stream of Blood," etc.; Thoro Harris, who wrote "All That Thrills My Soul Is Jesus," "He's Coming Soon," "More Abundantly," "By His Stripes We Are Healed," "Pentecost in My Soul," "Jesus Loves the Little Children," and other favorites.
[5] Howard Goss places the date even earlier. He speaks of "an association of ministers called 'Church of God in Christ' to which a few of us belonged from 1910-1914, mainly for purposes of business" (*op. cit.,* p. 163).

of Hot Springs, Arkansas; and D. C. O. Opperman constitute the new credentials committee.

During the summer of 1913, while attending the Interstate Camp Meeting at Eureka Springs, Arkansas, M. M. Pinson, editor of *Word and Witness*, and E. N. Bell, editor of *Apostolic Faith*, decided to join forces. Taking the name of the former and the format of the latter, Bell began publishing the *Word and Witness* at Malvern. Subsequent issues speak of the Church of God in Christ and gradually omit reference to the Apostolic Faith group. An advertisement in the October 20, 1913 issue urges all ministers of "The Churches of God in Christ" to report their ordination papers so as to be included in the official list for clergy certificates. Thus, it would appear that by late 1913 this organization had taken definite shape. The same issue announced the establishment of a "Bureau of Information" for the purpose of supplying authentic information from the field. The Bureau, headed by Bell, consisted of Robert Brown, New York City; Mrs. William Piper (*Latter Rain Evangel*) of Chicago; B. B. Stubb (?), Los Angeles; and A. H. Argue of Long Beach, California.

Perhaps a few names of the better known men out of the 352 in the Church of God in Christ will indicate the influence the group had on the Assemblies of God: Clyde Bailey, "Mother" Mary Barnes, Harry Bowley, Herbert Buffum, Hugh Cadwalder, A. B. Cox, W. T. Gaston, John Goben, C. A. Lasater, Agnes Ozman LaBerge, B. F. Lawrence, Fred Lohman, Burt McCafferty, Jacob Miller, M. M. Pinson, L. E. Riley, J. W. Welch, and R. E. Winsett.[6]

However, this was merely "an association of ministers ... we had no organization beyond a 'gentleman's agreement,' with the understanding for withdrawing of fellowship from the untrustworthy."[7] While a step in the right direction, it was obvious to the great majority of its members that the association was wholly inadequate, and

it was becoming increasingly apparent that something would have to be done, if we were to preserve the work. New situations were arising all the time, as our work grew larger and more unwieldy. New attitudes were needed.

As there was no apparent way to gather up the reins of the different cliques which seemed in danger of galloping off each in its own direction, Brother Bell and I worked privately together on

---

[6] *The Early History of the Assemblies of God*, pp. 6, 7, 8. David Hastie, a comparatively young man, startled the delegates at the 1959 General Council in San Antonio by stating that he believed he had attended every General Council. His voice was heard loud and clear at Hot Springs as he wailed in his mother's arms.

[7] Goss, *op. cit.*, p. 163

some kind of solution. We later found that Brother Opperman saw this need, too, as did a few others.

We realized that great care was needed at this stage, as we had been strictly taught against any form of organization. Irresponsible brethren, if they heard too much, might immediately use the opportunity to poison the saints against us before we could explain, and call us "compromisers!"—a serious charge in those days.

Of necessity, we secretly discussed calling a Conference to organize the work. So in November of 1913, Brother Bell and I ventured to announce a Conference at Hot Springs, Arkansas, from April 2 to 12, 1914. We signed the original call ourselves.

I say "ventured" advisedly, because we knew that we were likely facing serious opposition, unless God worked mightily. But other leaders took their stand with us, and added their names to the call, which was being published month by month in the *Word and Witness*. I don't think any of us had many rigid ideas as to how all this should be worked out, but we all supported system against the threatened chaos of the moment. Among other leaders there still seemed to be apprehension as to our purpose. In spite of all, we stuck to our guns and prayed. This took courage, but it seemed we had a special filling of grace from the Lord, and we truly felt that He was leading.[8]

The sponsors soon discovered that their apprehensions were well grounded. To many of the readers of *Word and Witness,* their call for a convention of this kind smelled suspiciously of an attempt to establish an ecclesiastical organization. A storm of opposition arose, editorials appeared condemning the action, sermons were preached labeling the move as anti-Pentecostal and anti-scriptural. It stirred up a deep-seated emotional reaction to organization, which was so radical that it had, on one occasion, erupted in violence. "At Grand River, Iowa . . . some independent spirit deliberately burned up the Church book, containing roster, minutes, records, etc." [9] Evidently, this Pentecostal arsonist felt that such a book should suffer the fate meted out at Ephesus to other books of sorcery!

Hostility to organization stemmed chiefly from the treatment which many of these Pentecostalists had received from their former denominations. After giving years of service, they had been "cast out of the synagogue," charged with "departing from the faith." Consequently, the last

---
[8] *Ibid.,* pp. 163, 174, 175.
[9] Hastie, *op. cit.,* p. 65.

GENERAL CONVENTION OF PENTECOSTAL SAINTS AND CHURCHES OF GOD IN CHRIST

HOT SPRINGS, ARKANSAS, APRIL 2 TO 12, 1914.

We desire at this time to make this preliminary announcement of this general meeting so that workers far and near, at home and abroad, may sidetrack everything else and be present. Laymen as well as preachers are invited. Especially do we urge all elders, pastors, ministers, evangelists and missionaries to be present. This call is to all the churches of God in Christ, to all Pentecostal or Apostolic Faith Assemblies who desire with united purpose to co-operate in love and peace to push the interests of the kingdom of God everywhere. This is, however, only for saints who believe in the baptism with the Holy Ghost with the sings following, Acts 2:4; 10:46; 19:6; Mark 16:16-18; 1 Cor. 12:8-11. Neither is this meeting for any captious, contrary, divisive or contentious person. But we leave for the body itself to take up any subjects it desires more than what is herein afterwards mentioned.

PURPOSES.

First—We come together that we may set a better understanding of what God would have us teach, that we may do away with so many divisions, both in doctrines and in the various names under which our Pentecostal people are working and incorporating. Let us come together as in Acts 15, to study the Word, and pray with and for each other—unity our chief aim.

Second—Again we come together that we know how to conserve the work, that we may all build up and not tear down, both in home and foreign lands.

Third—We come together for another reason, that we may get a better understanding of the needs of each foreign field, and may know how to place our money in such a way that one mission or missionary shall not suffer, while another not any more worthy, lives in luxuries. Also that we may discourage wasting money on those who are running here and there accomplishing nothing, and may concentrate our support on those who mean business for our King.

Fourth—Many of the saints have felt the need of chartering the churches of God in Christ, putting them on a legal basis, and thus *obeying the laws of the land,*" as God says. See Rom. 13. We confess we have been "slothful in business" on this point, and because of this many assemblies have already chartered under different names as a *local* work, in both home and foreign lands. Why not charter under *one Bible name,* 2 Thes. 2-14. Thus eliminating another phase of division in Pentecostal work? For this *purpose also let us* come together.

Fifth—We may also have a proposition to lay before the body for a general Bible Training School with a literary department for our people.

Now, brethren, as it is very important for all Pentecostal preachers to be present, you lay this before your people and get them to pay your fare to and fro. Winter tourist round trip tickets at cheap rates are on from nearly all over the country to Hot Springs up to April 30th, good to return up to June 1st, and you should buy these cheap round trip tickets. But if you fail in this, we want you to come anyhow, and if you have not faith to get home after you are here, then we will stand with you in trusting God for your return fare or to get out on the field. As we feel this General Assembly will do much good in spreading this glorious gospel around the world, we ask all the saints everywhere to send offerings to Financial Secretary H. A. Goss, Hot Springs, Ark., for the expenses of the meeting. In this way only can entertainment be provided. As far as possible let all come prepared to care for their own expenses.

The meeting will be held in the old Grand Opera House on Central Avenue, Hot Springs, Ark.

Many have expressed a desire for such a general meeting and it is with the encouragement of all these that we call this assembly. Only to get the matter before the brethren at once do the undersigned make the formal call. We expect to add the names of other brethren later. Let the leaders send their names to E. N. Bell, Malvern, Ark., to go on this list below.

The scope of the meeting may be enlarged as the Lord shall lead the brethren to do so. Meetings will go on day and night for the good of the saints.

M. M. Pinson, Phoenix, Ariz.
A. P. Collins, Ft. Worth, Tex.
H. A. Goss, Hot Springs, Ark.
D. C. O. Opperman, Houston, Texas.
E. N. Bell, Malvern, Ark.

thing they wanted in Pentecost was an ecclesiastical system
with its "shibboleths" and its hierarchy which could sum-
marily excommunicate them from Pentecostal ranks. One
iconoclast in Cumberland, Maryland, during a debate concerning organization, warned his brethren: "Beloved, I've
been listening to all that my brothers have said, and I feel
before God that we are on the wrong track. God has
brought us out of Popery, and, for Jesus' sake, let's not go
back in!" [10]

Regimentation was the thing that these refugees from
denominationalism greatly feared. They had "come out"
from creedal bondage and hierarchical denomination, and
they were determined to resist any efforts to cheat them
of their hard-won liberty. Voices were raised in protest
against putting so much harness upon the Pentecostal
horse that he could no longer pull (a well-understood
metaphor in those days). It was alleged that reliance upon
the might and power of ecclesiastical machinery would
replace reliance upon the Spirit of God, that denominational
pride would cause its members to concentrate on building
a "kingdom of this world," to the detriment of the spiritual
kingdom.

Fortunately, these arguments were not brushed aside as
groundless. None of the brethren who desired a simple
form of organization was so forgetful of his own painful
experience with ecclesiasticism that he shrugged off the
fears of the die-hard opponents of organization. "It could
happen here," as it had happened elsewhere, for Pentecostal
flesh is no more infallible than other flesh: all flesh is
flesh. Nevertheless, it was not organization itself which
was feared, but the abuse of organization. American
colonists had acknowledged the excellence of English law,
but had revolted against the tyrannous manner in which
George III had ignored that law. When the Revolution
proved successful and the colonists were forced to form
a government they built upon the principles of the law
under which they would have been content to live, if it had
been administered properly. So Pentecostalists would have

---

[10] Quoted by Walter C. Long, personal interview.

to learn to discriminate between organization and the evils which may (but not necessarily do) attend it.

Independency also had its evils. The situation which had prompted the announcement of a convention could not be attributed to organization, but to the extreme independence which prevailed. It was not a question of "too much harness": there was no harness at all on this Pentecostal horse! Doctrinal instability, cliques grouped around outstanding leaders, chaotic conditions in local assemblies, failure to conform to the laws of the state concerning ownership of property, etc., no check upon unscrupulous men at home and abroad: these things were grieving the hearts of men who sincerely loved the Movement.

One brother told how he had given his life to the building up of a work, souls being born through much toil and crying to God. But in a few days one with a hobby came in, and split wide open that which the pastor had been months and years in building. Souls for whom he had travailed in birth were thrown into confusion. For this reason he welcomed a cooperation that would help him save his flock from a similar disruption.[11]

Legitimate protection was needed for all such assemblies, it was argued. First, there should be a standard of ethical conduct to which all true men of God would be happy to subscribe. Second, there should be a doctrinal standard— not in the sense of a voluminous creed, but a simple statement concerning what the Pentecostal Movement approved as basic scriptural truths, and the teachings which it disapproved as unscriptural. This would not be an imposition of something entirely new. Local pastors and their assemblies already had such standards of doctrine and conduct, and this was simply an extension of those standards to all the assemblies. Definitely, there was a scriptural precedent for such action. The associations which had already been functioning, such as, the Church of God in Christ, had not proved adequate, but at least they had issued credentials only to those who, by their Pentecostal doctrine and righteous conduct, merited them.

The term *Bible Order*, was the slogan employed most

---

[11] Quoted in the *Latter Rain Evangel*, December, 1916.

often by those who favored organization. They firmly believed that the Bible taught that God was a God of order. The Pentecostal Movement had nothing to fear, in complying with 1 Corinthians 14:40: "Let all things be done decently and in order." Both in nature and in the history of His dealings with man, God is revealed by the Scriptures as the Initiator of organization. He made man gregarious by giving him physical birth into the human family, and spiritual birth into the spiritual family. Does not every family need some form of organization?

Old Testament saints were certainly organized, even though led supernaturally by the pillar and cloud. Human leadership existed in that theocratic era, each tribe having its elders and its position around the tabernacle and in the line of march, and over the entire twelve tribes, was the central direction of Moses and Joshua. Israel was not organized to depart from the cloud, but that it might follow the cloud! Through this divinely instituted organization, the Church in the wilderness was transformed from a downtrodden multitude of slave laborers into a tightly knit army which could march over some of the most desolate country in the world, care for the women and children en route, and triumph over its enemies.

The New Testament Church also had its own organization. The Holy Spirit who was the active agent of the Godhead in directing the saints of God bestowed the gift of "governments." In Acts 6 we see nominations, voting, officers, and church records. We note that the strong central church in Jerusalem exercised an oversight in the affairs of other assemblies (Acts 8, 15); that the apostles supervised churches over a wide area (Titus 1:5). While the apostles and the church in Jerusalem were unique, the supervisory system which they inaugurated was not confined to their day alone, but was meant to be exercised wherever the need for supervision existed.

It should not be inferred that the brethren who desired organization were contemplating a pyramiding hierarchy which imposed its will upon helpless ministers and congregations. They simply believed that each assembly should feel a responsibility toward the movement as a whole. No assembly liveth unto itself, nor can it separate itself from the other assemblies without violating an essential unity. As a member in a congregation has an individual responsibility to God and also a responsibility to his fellow believers, similarly the sovereignty of the local assembly does not cancel its obligation to other assemblies with which in a vital union it can establish and maintain standards of righteousness and faith.

Furthermore, it was asserted, the purpose of the Pentecostal Movement will be accelerated, not frustrated, by organization. What cannot be done individually can be done unitedly. Bible schools, publishing ventures, missionary efforts—all can be better served through our being "laborers together." The associations that have existed until now, while a step in the right direction, have not been adequate. We need to come together for a Council, to discuss what form of fellowship will be best for us. We shall not convene to legislate burdens which are impossible and galling, but, through prayer and discussion, to reach an understanding which is acceptable to all. Something must be done, and when something *must* be done, we know that God will help us to find the right solution. Safeguards against the evils of organization will be established, and yet a system of Bible order will be placed into operation to which all can repair.[12]

----

[12] These arguments concerning organization are taken from periodicals of the era and from personal reminiscences of men who advanced them at the time.

CHAPTER **2**

"THE FOUNDING FATHERS"

Some came hoping to block us. Others to back us up. None of us could unerringly read each other's heart or mind. So the first few days of prayer, praise and worship were also days of tension and suspicion. No one seemed to want to express his ideas first. Sometimes old friends were even ignored for fear of being seen talking to a "compromiser." [1]

Apparently, many of the preachers and laymen who answered the call to the famed resort of Hot Springs, Arkansas, deemed this convention "a case of last resort." But they came, "between 200 and 300" of them, maneuvering their venerable Fords over the ruts and out of the mud holes, fording the swollen streams, or swallowing the dust of a speeding Stutz Bearcat. Some travelled in "luxurious" trains into whose windows poured smoke and cinders! Others journeyed via horse and buggy, and the hardiest souls came to town astride "shank's mare." From twenty states and several foreign countries the pilgrims wended their way to the Grand Opera House on Central Avenue.

The First General Council was opened by a lengthy devotional service: three days and three nights of meetings —"for the good of the saints." It was not felt best to launch immediately into business! One happy discovery made by the attendants was that the Heavenly Dove had not been frightened away by the express purpose of the convention to effect some form of organization. The preachers gave forth their messages under a heavy anointing, the testimonies of the delegates concerning the out-

---
[1]   Goss, op. cit., p. 175.

pouring of the Spirit upon their fields of ministry caused all to rejoice, and the signal blessing of God upon the entire three days proved to the bitterest foes of organization that, thus far, at least, no steps had been taken which had caused the glory to depart.

Perhaps the greatest good accomplished by these three days was that an opportunity was provided for the delegates to get acquainted with one another. All sections of the country, with the exception of the extremely independent West Coast, had sent representatives to the Council. Broad "a" accents of New England mingled with soft Texan drawl and Midwestern twang. Many shades of Protestantism lurked in the background of these men and women, but now they formed a sort of "United Denominations," fused by a baptism of fire into a single Pentecostal body. How happily they sang:

> One of them, one of them,
> I am glad that I can say
> I'm one of them!

These three days, then, were not a mere prelude to the important business of setting up an organization; rather, they were the epitome of the basic theme of the Assemblies of God: "a voluntary, cooperative fellowship." *The fellowship does not exist because of the organization, but the organization exists because of the fellowship.* Getting acquainted with fellow Pentecostal believers and workers, learning to appreciate the vision which God has given them and the work He is doing through them, preserving and enlarging this fellowship: this is the true meaning of the Assemblies of God. The "about 120" registered delegates and the other attendants were engaged in far more than "preliminaries" when they took three days to extend to one another "the right hand of fellowship."

It might be a good idea for us to get acquainted with this illustrious group, at least, with the men who were to make outstanding contributions to the formation of the Assemblies of God. To many of the succeeding generations these men are only names in the official records.

What were they really like? What was their background?
What specific contribution did each man make in this
initial Council?

E. N. BELL

The Bighearted Chairman

The first Chairman of the Assemblies of God was
recognized as a leader in the Pentecostal Movement from
the moment he received the Spirit's fullness in 1907.
Eudorus N. Bell and his equally euphoniously named twin
brother, Endorus, were born in Lake Butler, Florida, on
June 27, 1866. The whole family knew hardship from the
time that the father died when the boys were only two
years old. Eudorus was converted at an early age and
received a call into the ministry.

Realizing his need of training, he chose the John B.
Stetson University in De Land, Florida, and started "working his way through college." It was a struggle. When the
exchequer was lower than usual, Bell bought stale bread,
soaked it in water, and meal after meal learned to "live
by bread alone." His theological training was received at
the Baptist Seminary in Louisville, Kentucky, and three
years of further graduate study were spent at the University of Chicago. For seventeen years he served as a pastor
in the Southern Baptist Convention, his last pastorate being
in Fort Worth, Texas. His Pentecostal experience cost him
his relationship with the Baptist churches, but he found
a warm welcome waiting him among Pentecostal people,
and he ministered in various assemblies through the South.
As Bell came to the Hot Springs Council, he was the
pastor of a strong assembly of 250 adherents in Malvern,
Arkansas, and editor of the influential *Word and Witness*.
E. N. Bell was a modest man. He did not seek to impress
his self-taught brethren with his academic background.
Delightfully simple in his speaking and writing, he was
the man who, in the early years, helped the Movement
as a whole to understand the principles of the Assemblies
of God. He was always careful to be fair, never "bull-
dogmatic," and scarcely ever given to impetuous action
(evidenced by his remaining a bachelor until reaching the

advanced age of 43!), yet thoughtful enough to have convictions, and intensely loyal to Pentecostal truth. In other words, E. N. (which he preferred to "Eudorus"!) Bell was an ideal chairman for this first General Council.

HOWARD A. GOSS
The Ardent Promoter

The man who was chiefly responsible for the Hot Springs Council was only thirty years old, but already a Pentecostal veteran. Howard A. Goss was an instinctive reporter and has preserved many authentic memories of the early days which otherwise would be lost. A fine evangelist, Howard Goss established numerous thriving churches (Malvern, Arkansas, for example). He was one of the first to see the need of tying together all of the struggling and widely separated assemblies, and prodded the slower-moving Bell into publishing the announcement of the first Council. His lease upon the Grand Opera House, his rallying of his own Hot Springs congregation to entertain the delegates, and his serving as "financial secretary" were major factors in launching the young organization.

J. W. WELCH
The Steadying Influence

John William Welch waited until he was forty to accept ordination. Feeling himself unqualified for the ministry, Welch had devoted himself to establishing Sunday schools for the American Sunday School Union, to street meetings, and Gospel mission services. At the General Electric plant in Schenectady, New York, where he was employed, Welch was engaged in a soul-saving ministry. While attending a Christian and Missionary Alliance convention in Nyack, New York, in 1899, Welch was told by the leaders, "You are qualified for ordination, and we are going to ordain you."

In 1910 he was sent to "superintend" the Alliance work in Oklahoma, but soon discovered that he was the only Alliance preacher in the state. Conducting services every night for six months in the town of Muskogee brought a harvest of souls, and yet Welch was hungry for a deeper experience with God. When a band of Pentecostal pioneers, led by A. B. Cox, came to Muskogee, he was convinced of his need for the Pentecostal baptism, which he received a few months later. Shortly after, W. T. Gaston, pastor of the Tahlequah, Oklahoma, assembly, invited Welch to come for a revival campaign, and from that time Welch was a Pentecostal preacher.

"Daddy" Welch (as he was affectionately called) was a man of integrity. In committee sessions he helped to direct policy into the paths of righteousness by remarks such as these: "This is clearly the righteous thing to do. Let us do it, and trust God. . . . " And, "This is God's money. We must use it with wisdom and care. The handling of funds entrusted to our care by the people of God is a sacred responsibility." [2] Welch was also a keen judge of human nature, as is illustrated by his admonition to Fred Vogler in 1919. A man rushed up to Welch to tell his side of a controversy, and when he left, Welch turned to Vogler and said, "Remember this, Fred, the man who gets in the 'first wedge' isn't always right."

Strong-minded, balanced, and dignified, Welch was indeed a steadying influence upon this first Council and subsequent Councils as well. But he would never have been accepted as an elder to whom the younger brethren (and at least 80 per cent were quite youthful) could turn for counsel, unless he had also been "a man of the Spirit." At one convention, the meeting was exceptionally dry and the sense of bondage was oppressive. Sitting on the platform, Welch felt suddenly impressed to rise to his feet, turn completely around, and sit down again. He argued briefly about the foolishness of this impression, but the Lord convinced him that it was from Him and certainly it was no more foolish than some of the strange actions commanded the prophets of old. Welch obeyed. The congregation was startled for such a man to act thus, but then, realizing that he had been willing to be made "a fool" to see the Spirit of God move in the

---

[2] *Pentecostal Evangel*, July 29, 1939.

meeting, they, too, opened their hearts to the Lord and forgot man and his opinions. The meeting that was bound hand and foot was loosed! This obedience to the Spirit of God was a "must" to an early day leader, and J. W. Welch qualified.

J. ROSWELL FLOWER [3]
The Perennial Secretary

Only twenty-six at Hot Springs, J. Roswell Flower was the youngest of the leaders. Born in 1888 in Canada, the son of godly parents, Flower studied law in Indianapolis. His conversion in 1907 and his reception of the fullness of the Spirit two years later changed the direction of his life into the ministry, but his knowledge of the law was to prove invaluable in the years to come. Ordained at a Pentecostal camp meeting in Plainfield, Indiana, by D. W. Myland, he received credentials from the World's Faith Missionary Association and began to pastor a small church in Indianapolis. At the same time he published a weekly paper, *the Christian Evangel,* the first weekly periodical to be published in the Pentecostal Movement.

You will notice that, in the Hot Springs picture, Flower is just about in the middle of the leaders kneeling in the forefront. Ever since that hour, he has been in the middle of the leaders! Probably no other man has been so closely identified with the Assemblies of God as J. Roswell Flower. He has been a key man through the years. Alert, intelligent, energetic, fearlessly Pentecostal, he was a natural choice as the secretary, a post he was to fill for a total of twenty-seven years (1914-16 and 1935-1959) in all. Flower has been active in every phase of the ministry, serving in every district and general council office but that of the Chairman (or General Superintendent). He served as the first full-time Foreign Missions Secretary from 1919 to 1925. He is the only man who has attended all the General Councils from the beginning in 1914 to the present time. His total contribution to the Assemblies of God is at least the equal of that of any other man. All five of his children are in the ministry—a factor to be

---

[3] Flower died in 1970 at the age of 82. His son, Joseph R. Flower, was elected secretary in 1975.

taken into consideration in gauging the ministry of this
remarkable man.

M. M. PINSON
The Fiery Keynoter

The keynote address at Hot Springs was given by M. M.
Pinson, a former Holiness preacher from Tennessee. He
used the fifteenth chapter of the Acts of the Apostles as a
guide for the deliberations of the first General Council of
the Assemblies of God. What sort of man was this
Tennessean who was chosen to preach the first sermon,
which in reality struck a keynote, and was well received by
the entire convention? Pinson was a good solid Bible
preacher, whose trademark in the meeting was a quick,
high-pitched "Amen!" He wore a built-up heel to compen-
sate for the shortness of one leg. Active in the founding
of the white "Church of God in Christ," a former editor
of *Word and Witness,* Pinson was also to become one of
the first workers among the Latin Americans and the
American Indians.

Pinson was a fighter, not for personal advantage, but
for principles in which he believed. Job's description of the
warhorse (39:22, 25) fits this man: "He mocketh at
fear, and is not affrighted, neither turneth he back from
the sword . . . he saith among the trumpets, ha, ha; and he
smelleth the battle afar off, the thunder of the captains,
and the shouting." Pinson was an articulate man with
convictions who had a definite influence upon the delegates at this and subsequent early Councils—a good man
to have on your side!

T. K. LEONARD
A Foundation Stone

Thomas K. Leonard was one of the giants during the
formative days of the Assemblies of God. Ordained in the
Christian Church in 1901, and re-ordained after his Pentecostal experience by his own church, "the Assembly of
God," in Findlay, Ohio, in 1912, Leonard was a successful
pastor and revivalist. Men who watched him in action on
the Council floor say that Leonard would have made a

good lawyer. His career was rather paradoxical: essentially a "lone wolf," T. K. Leonard was an individualist who found it difficult to work with a team, yet he was a vigorous supporter of church order. No one can deny that this man who gave the Assemblies of God its first Constitutional preamble and resolution, its official name, and the name of its publishing house, deserves to have his name inscribed upon the foundation of the Movement.

ARCH P. COLLINS

The Saintly Peacemaker

This man was one of the sweetest spirited men in Pentecostal history—our "John Fletcher."

He was loved by all who knew his great heart. Little children loved to take his hand, and those who had grown gray with the frost of many winters were glad to feel his friendly clasp. Many a young preacher will bless the God of Heaven for Brother Collins, for he often led them forward and with his arm around them in the presence of the people would ask prayer for them. Many a young preacher has felt a hand slip into his coat pocket, only to find later that it was a one, five, or ten dollar bill put there by this dear man of God. . . .

He was an invaluable man at the meetings of the General Council. When he saw the tendency of some to legislate for everything, he would sound out a warning. Brother Welch whispered at one Council meeting: "Collins is a faithful watchdog." He was quick to scent danger. He stood firmly for the "larger fellowship" of all the bloodwashed, and had absolutely no sympathy for the spirit that wants to disfellowship everyone who does not see everything from the identical viewpoint. He was the embodiment of the General Council in this spirit. [4]

E. N. Bell reveals one source of the sweetness and saintliness of this "son of consolation":

In 1914 at the Council meeting in Chicago he and I roomed together. Almost every morning he awakened me with his praying and worshiping in the adjoining room. It was not merely a matter of getting something from God. It was a time of great fellowship between his soul and heaven. He would often seem lost in adoration and praise to God[5]

---

[4] *Pentecostal Evangel*, July 9, 1921.   [5] *Ibid.*

D. C. O. OPPERMAN
The Pioneer Educator

Daniel Opperman was a key figure in the Pentecostal Movement from the moment he resigned his post as principal of the school system in Zion City, Illinois, to seek the fullness of the Spirit. Ill health was also a factor in this decision, for he had contracted tuberculosis. While praying for the baptism of the Spirit in Houston, Opperman felt impressed to go out on the streets and preach Christ, even though his physical condition militated against strenuous activity, especially open-air preaching. Nevertheless, he decided to step out on the promise of God—and was instantly healed!

Several "oldtimers," including H. M. Cadwalder and Howard A. Goss, have mentioned Opperman's sensitivity to the Spirit of God, his sympathy and understanding. These qualities were of inestimable value in his Bible school work.

He trained and put hundreds of workers into the Pentecostal harvest field. His schools were a "cutting out" station also, where those not called to active evangelism could painlessly find it out without regrets. These were safely channeled into other lines of God's service. For many years he was a handsome and commanding figure amongst us, full of faith and of the Holy Ghost." [6]

Much of Opperman's work was not of the type that commands headlines, but his contribution to the discussions and his ability to lift others into the Spirit proved to be of real significance to the Assemblies of God. It will be noted that his name appears as an endorser of the "Call." In recognition of his ministry within the fellowship Opperman was named the first Assistant Chairman in the Chicago Council of 1914.

* * *

Five Chairmen (later, Superintendents) were present at the first General Council: E. N. Bell, A. P. Collins, J. W. Welch, W. T. Gaston, and R. M. Riggs. Among other outstanding men in attendance were John G. Lake,

[6] *Goss, op. cit.,* p. 128.

F. F. Bosworth, Jacob Miller, A. B. Cox, E. N. Richey, R. E. Erdman, S. A. Jamieson, Fred Pitcher, B. F. Lawrence, Cyrus B. Fockler, J. Roswell Flower, and John Sinclair.

The Assemblies of God has not experienced a prodigious growth simply through "a fortuitous concourse of atoms," a blind and nondirected evolution. God has set in this Revival Movement "governments," men who, under divine guidance, have molded its character. Their sound, spiritual and progressive leadership has been a major factor in lifting the Assemblies of God in less than fifty years from an obscure and despised Pentecostal sect into world prominence.

CHAPTER 3

THE SECRET COMMITTEE'S REPORT

THE INITIAL business meeting of the First General Council of the Assemblies of God was called to order on Monday, April 6, 1914. E. N. Bell, the acting chairman, was asked by the entire convention to serve as chairman for all of the sessions, and J. R. Flower was elected as secretary. Since there was no agenda, the first order of business was the appointment by the chairman of a committee whose duty was "to receive from all the brethren present the subjects desired discussed, and to arrange and present them in the form of suitable reports and resolutions to the convention." [1] The committee was a representative body, selected on a regional basis.

While this large committee was in session, a smaller, self-appointed committee with its own ideas of what constituted "suitable reports and resolutions," caucused secretly, under the leadership of T. K. Leonard of Findlay, Ohio. Goss comments:

One night a group of opposition [well meaning] ministers met privately and formed a resolution to be brought to the floor—a resolution which they hoped would forestall any move on our part toward rigid organization. Some of them knew that we wanted to incorporate with rules and regulations, and this knowledge, perhaps, aroused their suspicion. [2]

Undoubtedly, this is a correct analysis of the motive which inspired this committee, but it would be as inaccurate to infer from the comment that all the members of this committee were anti-organization as it would be

---

[1] *Minutes.*   [2] Goss, *op. cit.*, p. 176.

to infer that all of the members of the first committee were pro-organization. Honest differences of opinion existed within both committees, causing "heated discussion" far into the night. The "Call" for this Council had made it clear that "any captious, contrary, divisive or contentious person" would not be welcome, but full and free debate was encouraged.

M. M. Pinson had pointed out in his sermon that at the Jerusalem Council (Acts 15) the early Christians, by harmonizing the seemingly irreconcilable views and removing the causes of friction, safely welded together the Jewish and Gentile Church. However, this blessed result was not achieved without "much disputing." Is not this freedom to express divergent views embodied in the very word "Council"? Its root meaning indicates that it is a time to counsel, to discuss, to consider. But while much discussion occurred, a great deal of this spring night was spent in "effectual, fervent prayer." Jacob Miller, a member of the second committee, at a later Council "reminded the brethren how eight of them got together and prayed at Hot Springs, and how the Preamble to Constitution was literally prayed forth." [3]

Toward the wee hours of the morning, T. K. Leonard, the chairman of the second committee, began to summarize and to systematize the arguments pro and con, and to dictate to Flower a report and resolution for presentation to the convention the next day. The whole committee approved the writing, and turned wearily toward bed. Big things were coming on the morrow.

In the meantime, someone got wind that the secret committee had been working, with the result that representatives of that committee were invited to meet with the regularly appointed committee for an understanding. At first some resentment was manifested, but when Leonard drew from his pocket the document that had been prepared and read it, the resentment vanished, for the members of the first committee discovered they were in full accord with the principles expressed therein. The first committee

---

[3] *Pentecostal Evangel*, October 10, 1925.

had not progressed in its thinking as far as the secret committee, but now that this document had been prepared, even though in an unorthodox manner, they were ready to consider it for presentation on the floor of the Council.

Bighearted E. N. Bell, chairman of the first committee, proved on this occasion that he was not one to hold resentment, nor would he insist on protocol. Goss recalls that he "leaned across to me and whispered, 'Brother Goss, they have the very thing we need and want!' I joyfully agreed." [4] Bell stood to his feet at the conclusion of the reading of the resolution, and exclaimed, "Brethren, herein is a marvelous thing! Without any collusion whatsoever—in fact, (and a twinkle appeared in his eyes) we didn't even know that these brethren were meeting, the two committees have reached almost exactly the same conclusions concerning the purpose of this convention and the type of association which should bind this group of Pentecostal believers together. If I may have just a moment to confer with the brethren of the first committee, I am confident that they will concur in this statement of mine, and perhaps even be willing to forego their own resolution and to cosponsor the resolution which has been so ably presented to us this morning."

The members of the larger committee, interested only in effective action, happily gave their consent, with the result that the report became recognized as the work of the combined committees, and was presented to the floor of the convention with their approval by T. K. Leonard, who never had a more attentive audience, as he read slowly and distinctly the following:

A DECLARATION OF INDEPENDENCE

1. That God, our heavenly Father, sent His only-begotten Son into the world who built and established His church upon the foundation of the apostles and prophets, Jesus Christ Himself being the Head and Chief Corner Stone.

2. That the holy inspired Scriptures are the all-sufficient rule for faith and practice, and we shall not add to or take from them.

3. That Christ commanded that there should be no schism in His Body, the General Assembly and Church of the first born, which are written in Heaven.

---

[4] Goss, *op. cit.*, p. 176.

4. That we recognize ourselves as members of said Assembly of God and do not believe in identifying ourselves into a sect or denomination which constitutes an organization which legislates or forms laws and articles of faith and has jurisdiction over its members and creates unscriptural lines of fellowship and disfellowship, which separates itself from other members of the General Assembly of the first born.[5]

It was clear that these Pentecostal believers did not desire to start a church. The convention was being called upon to recognize that the Church had already been established by Christ, and that all true believers are members of that Church.

Leonard's declaration was somewhat unrealistic, for if all of its sentiments had been put into effect, little could have been accomplished in resolving the problem of the hour. Nevertheless, it expressed the independent beliefs of the delegates. It was a statement of intent. If it erred in any direction, it was far better to err on the side of freedom—not merely because it found unanimous agreement at that particular time, but because it provided a foundation for the whole philosophy of church government in the Assemblies of God. Liberal interpretations were to be given to these words in later years, but the spirit embodied therein was to be preserved to the present hour.

A DECLARATION OF DEPENDENCE

Something concrete by way of resolution had to be offered. Leonard and company were ready with that, too. The following resolution, though on the negative side, did reveal the dependence of each assembly upon each other, and consequently, proposed definite organizational steps:

Resolved, First, That we recognize that we have assembled as a general council of Pentecostal saints from local Churches of God in Christ, Assemblies of God, and various Apostolic Faith Missions and Churches, and Full Gospel Pentecostal Missions, and assemblies of like faith in the United States and foreign lands, whose purpose is not to legislate laws of government, nor to usurp authority over said various assemblies, nor to deprive them of their scriptural rights and privileges.

Second, to recognize scriptural methods and rules of unity, fellow-

---

[5] *Minutes.*

ship, work and business for God, and to disapprove all unscriptural methods and conduct, endeavoring to keep the unity of the faith and of the knowledge of the Son of God, unto a perfect man, unto the measure of the stature of the fulness of Christ, and to walk accordingly (Eph. 4:1-32).

Finally, That we recognize all of the above said assemblies of various names, and, when speaking of them, refer to them by the general scriptural name, i.e., "Assembly of God," and adopt it as soon as possible for the purpose of convenience, unity, fellowship, and to be more scriptural and legal in transacting business, owning property, and executing missionary work at home and foreign lands.[*]

At the conclusion of the reading of the report, a rising tide of rejoicing caught up the entire body of delegates. When the vote was taken it proved unanimous. The meeting of minds was a definite indication of the leading of the Holy Spirit. Utterances in tongues and their interpretation and prophecy confirmed this belief. A great wave of joy and thanksgiving swept over the congregation. Even the most skeptical could feel the approval of God upon what was being done. As at the General Council in Jerusalem, these delegates discovered that the Spirit of Glory had not departed from them in their Council business. He was still alongside to help, so that they might say, "It seemed good to the Holy Ghost and to us!"

What relief was felt by these Spirit-filled believers who had been brought out of hidebound denominationalism and who had looked askance at any suggestion of parliamentary procedure, resolutions, etc., which might obstruct the freedom of the Spirit! They had become restive when the Council took on business forms, but these same people had chafed under the lack of system which had prevailed up until this time. In order to correct the one extreme, it was necessary to have a semblance of the other, but they were discovering that there was a happy medium between the two extremes. Divine order had not brought bondage but true freedom and harmony.

This first Council has been called the "Constitutional Convention," but this is a misnomer, for no constitution

---
[*] *Ibid.*

was adopted at Hot Springs. The resolution that was adopted was incorporated into the Preamble, but the Constitution itself was not to make its appearance until 1927. Neither was a Statement of Faith adopted. Yet, the following actions that were taken at this time helped to lay the foundation for the polity of the Assemblies of God:

1. That the General Council of the Assemblies of God be incorporated.

2. That all business formerly undertaken in the Interstate Camp Meeting of the Churches of God in Christ at Eureka Springs, Ark., be now committed to the General Council of the Assemblies of God.

3. That the monthly *Word and Witness* and the weekly *Christian Evangel* become the official organs of the Assemblies of God.

4. That local assemblies in given areas be authorized to form district or state councils, in harmony with the principles and purposes of the General Council.

5. That recognition be given to the various ministries of elder, evangelist, minister, exhorter and deacon, together with recognition of the ministries of women.

6. That divorce and remarriage be discouraged, and that ministerial credentials be withheld from divorced persons who remarry.

7. That extreme teachings concerning the eating of meats be disapproved (Col. 2:14-17).

8. That Thursday be recognized and encouraged as a weekly day of prayer.

9. That ministers be encouraged to avail themselves of training that could be received through correspondence courses and enrollment in the Bible schools then in existence.[7]

Bell and Flower were elected to continue to fill their posts of Chairman and Secretary, respectively. Their duties were, mainly, to arrange for and preside over the annual council meeting, to publish the minutes of the council sessions and to keep the Movement informed of Council activities throughout the year. Credentials in the name of the General Council of the Assemblies of God were to be given to "worthy ministers within the Pentecostal, Apostolic Faith and Church of God in Christ groups" who requested them. Howard Goss, of Hot Springs, Arkansas, was to issue the credentials to the ministers in the South and

---

[7] *Ibid.*

West, while T. K. Leonard was to dispense them in the
North and East.

The sole departure from absolute congregationalism
occurred when a resolution was passed authorizing the
appointment of twelve representative men "to act in all
necessary matters on behalf of this General Council as a
Home and Foreign Missionary and Executive Presbytery
during the ensuing year, or until their successors are appointed." Eight men were selected, and an additional four
were to be appointed on a sectional basis at a later date:
E. N. Bell, J. R. Flower, T. K. Leonard, H. A. Goss, J. W.
Welch, M. M. Pinson, C. B. Fockler, and D. C. O. Opperman. A. P. Collins, D. W. Kerr, and John Sinclair were
subsequently added to the list, but the twelfth man was not
appointed until the next Council.

While it is true that these twelve men were to serve only
in an advisory capacity, it did reveal that the delegates felt
the need for some form of central government. The word,
presbyter, is a good Bible term. Paul speaks of "the laying
on of hands of the presbytery" (1 Timothy 4:14) .

The Jewish council was composed of the elders of the Church (the
presbytery, Lk. 22:66; Acts 22:5) and a presiding rabbi; so the
Christian Church was composed of apostles, elders, and a president
(Acts 15:6, 13-21) .[8]

Presbuterion is the Greek word for presbytery, from
which, of course, is derived the word, Presbyterian. This
meant that the newly formed Assemblies of God was to
have a polity heritage from John Knox! Later, with the
advent of District Councils and the change from "chairman"
to "superintendent," as the supervisory work became a
necessity, we incorporated a phase of Methodism, *District
Superintendents.* We really have a hybrid-polity! Congregational, Baptist, Presbyterian, Methodist! This may not be
a fault, however; it may prove to be, like hybrids in other
realms, even better than the single strains, because it
takes the strong points of each system while seeking to
avoid its weaknesses. The glory of the Assemblies of
God is its nonconformity to any single polity.

---

[8] Jamieson, Fausset and Brown, p. 414.

Some can work well under one framework of church government, and some are more at ease under another. A few of our brother Pentecostal organizations have a modified Episcopalian polity, with a strong centralized leadership, which appoints pastors to churches, and requires each church to be directly responsible to headquarters. This system has worked beautifully for them, and they have prospered under it, with the blessing of the Lord resting richly upon them. But the climate at Hot Springs, and since, in the Assemblies of God would not permit any strong Episcopalian tendencies. There have been times when our leaders on a District level and General level must have felt frustrated by the slow working of the more democratic system, but it has, in the long run, proved best for us.

The brethren who laid the foundation of Assemblies of God polity would be positively awestruck and probably dismayed if they could behold the superstructure which has evolved through the years. The founding fathers of America might draw back in horror, too, if they were to be shown the gargantuan federal government of the twentieth century. But their horror would undoubtedly give way to delight, when they discovered that the republic still rests upon the foundation of individual liberty, that there is still "equal justice under the law," that Jeffersonian democracy has not been eclipsed by Hamiltonian authoritarianism, that "we the people" still rule "the land of the free and the home of the brave."

Similarly, the dismay the wise master builders who laid the foundations of the Assemblies of God might feel on returning after almost a half of a century would be offset by the discovery that the government is still on the shoulder of the Head of the Church, the Lord Jesus Christ. While supervisory leadership has been added as the need arose, no attempt has been made to force the local assemblies into one mold. The sovereignty of the local assembly is still inviolate. The indigenous principle which the Assemblies of God has so vigorously advocated in its missionary enterprise has been jealously guarded for the American assembly. There is a general pattern of polity, but this is combined with the freedom to express itself individually. For example, the great variety of names bestowed upon local assemblies! This freedom extends through every stratum of the General Council of the Assemblies of God, the District Councils, the ministers, and the members of the congregations.

Even the best system can be ill administered. The observation attributed to Abraham Lincoln is true: "The best way to find out what is in a man is to put him into office." The vast majority of men who have served on varying levels in the organization have been men of judgment and fair play. A few have abused the authority of their office, but the system of government instituted at Hot Springs has vindicated itself by dealing effectively with such men. The combination of individual liberty and "Bible Order" has stood every test for over sixty years, ample proof that the pioneers in the First General Council wrought in God.

CHAPTER **4**

"A GOOD NAME"

"A GOOD NAME is rather to be chosen than great riches."[1] One of the purposes of the call for a General Convention was

that we may do away with so many divisions ... in the various names under which our Pentecostal people are working and incorporating ... many assemblies have already chartered under different names, as a *local* work, in both home and foreign lands. Why not charter under one *Bible* name?[2]

"Assemblies of God," the name suggested by T. K. Leonard, of Findlay, Ohio, seemed to ring the bell. One point which recommended it to the delegates was that no other group had a prior claim to it, as in the case of "Apostolic Faith," "Church of God," and "Church of God in Christ." Its simplicity appealed to all foes of ecclesiastical pomp and ceremony. Other desirable features were that "Assemblies of God" was not derived from the name of any man; it was not a designation of a particular form of church government; it was not a reference to one particular doctrine held by the group.

Its chief attraction may well have been that it did not imply too much. Down through the centuries groups have adopted Biblical names which refer to *all* of the blood-washed, Spirit-regenerated children of God, the Universal Church, the Body of Christ. This practice is perfectly legitimate, as long as the group does not arrogate to itself the whole meaning of the name. Some tight little

---

[1] Proverbs 22:1.
[2] *Word and Witness*, December 20, 1913.

sects and some big ones became so proud of their choice of name, and so exclusive in their application of it, that they confused their group with the entire Church, asserting that one must belong to "the Church" to be saved, and such narrow sectarians always spoke of their organization as "the Church." This inversion is reminiscent of the fabled rooster who was convinced that the sun came up because he crowed!

The delegates at Hot Springs did not profess to have selected the only proper Bible name for the Church. There were a number of splendid scriptural titles for the Church which were already being employed. "Assemblies of God" is certainly not anti-scriptural, and definitely not unscriptural. Hebrews 12:23 was a text to which T. K. Leonard pointed as a basis for his selection: "The general assembly and church of the firstborn."

"Church" is more familiar than "assembly," and it would be foolish to discriminate against a word so loved and cherished by all Christendom. However, a fact that is obvious to all students of the Greek New Testament should be pointed out: viz., the actual word "church" does not appear in the Greek text. That it is so translated into English does not place it in the Greek. The derivation of church, like the Scotch *kirk* and the German *kircke,* is generally thought to be from the Greek *kuriakon,* "belonging to the Lord." It may be connected with the Latin word for "circle," *circus, circulus,* and the Greek *kuklos,* a reference to the congregation's gathering in circles. *Ekklesia* originally meant "an *assembly* called out by the magistrate or some other responsible official." It was in this sense that it was adopted from the secular and applied to the sacred by the New Testament writers, and undoubtedly this is the reason why many conservative Bible scholars demonstrate a fondness for the word "assembly," employing it often to describe the local congregation.

"Assemblies of God," in addition to being a scriptural name, expresses the very heart of the Pentecostal Movement, the emphasis upon the assembling of believers together in His name. The gathering together of the saints for worship, prayer, fellowship, preaching, testimony, and evangelism is the center of Pentecostal life. Too, the name is well suited to the organization created at Hot Springs, an affiliation of independent assemblies which are complete churches in themselves. It reflects the impersonal and un-sectarian nature of this co-operative fellowship.

Note that it is the "Assemblies of *God*." We must not lose sight of the transcendent element in the church. It is not a mere fraternal order, a social club, or a humanitarian organization resting upon human brotherhood, but a super-natural body, which traces its descent not from the first man but from the second man, who is "the Lord from heaven." Mere assembling would have no real meaning, if He were not "in the midst." The people of God are not and cannot be separated from God. We are nothing without God. We have been "called out" by God. We have been drawn together by a common purpose—God. All this is set forth in the name, "Assemblies of God."

A word or two now about the debit side of the name. For years, it was an unfamiliar appellation which drew only a blank look when it was mentioned. Many pastors and congregations who sought to comply with the recommenda-tion that all the assemblies associated with the fellowship should identify themselves by using the name felt that it was necessary to add the word "church": "Assembly of God *Church*." This was a redundancy which, after the name and its significance became better known, was re-moved from the official name of the local congregations. The problem of identifying an assembly of a variant name with the fellowship as a whole has been solved by appending the organizational name, "Assemblies of God."

One annoyance has been the unwieldiness of the complete name, "The General Council of the Assemblies of God." Did you ever try to write that on a questionnaire? It would appear that in the early days the words "General Council" were used predominantly when referring to the organiza-tion. Men spoke of "the General Council," or simply, "the Council." In more recent times these words have been dropped, except for official or legal purposes, in favor of "Assemblies of God." In ordinary speaking, "General

Council" has come gradually to mean the biennial conference, while "Assemblies of God" is now the popular
name for the Movement itself.

One last drawback we would mention is the confusion
that sometimes arises over the proper employment of the
singular or the plural form of the name. The singular,
"Assembly of God," is used in connection with the local
congregation. In an exceptional sense, the singular might
serve as a designation of the entire fellowship, but generally
speaking, the plural is the more correct and more apt
form. The official name of the association of various local
assemblies which was founded at Hot Springs, Arkansas,
is "The General Council of the *Assemblies* of God." When
speaking in a collective sense of the organization itself,
singular verbs, pronouns, etc. are used. When the reference
is to numerous individual assemblies, but not to the
organizational aspect, plural verbs, pronouns, etc. are to be
employed.

To anticipate chronological events, a word should be
said about an attempt to substitute another name for
"Assemblies of God." Some dissatisfaction was expressed
through the years, for the reasons which we have cited.
In the 1927 General Council a number of the brethren,
some of them executives, sought to change the name to
The Pentecostal Evangelical Church. This was a pleasant,
euphonious and fully descriptive name, and it included the
word "church." Strong pleas were entered for this change,
but the man who offered the original name to the first
General Council, T. K. Leonard, was too persuasive. The
name had become more familiar to the world at large.
Why change the name now, after it had taken so long to
make it known? Furthermore many of the local church
properties had been registered under the name "Assembly
of God." and to change the name of the organization to
some other name would involve the changing of titles
to church property. The motion to substitute was overwhelmingly defeated. This was the only serious attempt to
change the name, and in all probability it will be the last.

"A good name" was chosen by the delegates at the first
General Council, and we believe that the Lord in His

mercy guided them in their choice. But the fact that it was a good name to begin with, a Biblical name, is not the sole reason why it is universally regarded as a good name today, a name that is significant in the religious world. "Great riches" of sacrifice, spiritual life, talent, hard work, and unselfishness have made it the name it is today. May we who have inherited it, who are proud to own it, gladly contribute our share to the wealth signified by the good name "Assemblies of God."

CHAPTER **5**

"ON THE MOVE"

HIGH ON THE rocks in the upper left-hand corner of the picture of the first General Council is a young man whose face is strangely familiar. The son of a Mississippi surgeon, this lad, with his mother, had come into the light of Pentecost at the Bible school in Hattiesburg, Mississippi, in 1909, and was baptized in a Fort Worth, Texas, lake by Arch P. Collins in 1911. Although only eighteen at Hot Springs, he was already a keen observer, and his eyes did not miss a thing in that initial council. Turning one day to Lee Floyd, he remarked, "You know, I like this. I believe I'll stick with it!" [1] And he did stick with it, attending the Elim School in Rochester, New York, serving as a missionary in South Africa, as a Bible school instructor in the United States, a successful pastor, an outstanding author, a district superintendent, and the eighth General Superintendent of the Assemblies of God—*Ralph M. Riggs!*

The wonderful spirit and the solid achievements at Hot Springs caused hundreds of other Pentecostal believers to throw in their lot with the newly formed Council. Some denounced the work of the brethren, and prophesied doom for their presuming "to place restrictions on the moving of the Holy Ghost." But the reaction of most believers who scrutinized the accounts of the Council in the *Word and Witness* and the *Christian Evangel* (whose combined circulation had soared to 25,000 by August, 1914), was as favorable as that of the Antioch Christians to whom Barna-

---

[1] Letter from Lee Floyd to J. R. Flower, 1959.

bas and Paul delivered the report of the first General
Council in Jerusalem: "Which when they had read, they
rejoiced for the consolation." [2]

The first step for incorporation, as authorized by the
Council, was in Arkansas while E. N. Bell was still serving
as pastor of the Malvern Assembly and Howard A. Goss
was in Hot Springs.[3] The General Council was to be incorporated a second time, after the establishing of the
primitive headquarters in St. Louis, Missouri, in October,
1916. The General Council of the Assemblies of God, with
its District Councils being formed across the land, was "in
business." At this initial stage, however, it was definitely
small business.

T. K. Leonard (a truly indispensable man at Hot
Springs) had generously offered his small printing plant
and school property at Findlay, Ohio, to the young Movement, for the publication of its periodicals. Since both
space and equipment at Malvern, Arkansas, and Plainfield, Indiana, were inadequate, Bell and Flower decided
to combine their publishing interests and move to Findlay.
During their brief stay in that Ohio city, the two men
served on the faculty of the *Gospel School,* which Leonard
had established in connection with the local assembly.

The need for unity and protection in missionary endeavors had
been one of the great factors in the organization of the Assemblies
of God ... By the time the General Council was organized, there
were great numbers of missionaries already on the field. These
workers, in many instances, had buildings, homes, schools, and
other facilities. Support for such works was being received by means
of correspondence with friends in the United States. Many of
the missionaries joined the new fellowship and requested help.
The early missionary program, up to 1917, consisted largely in
publicizing the needs of the missionaries and forwarding what
money was available. Hence, Editor Bell wrote in the August 22,
1914, *Christian Evangel:*

"Because of this great circulation (25,000) our papers are
enabled to be strong agencies for the use of missionaries, carrying
the needs of the field direct to those in the homeland who
have some of the Lord's money, who in turn respond to
the need and send it to us to be forwarded, which we gladly

[2] Acts 15:31.
[3] *Goss, op. cit.,* p. 177.

do without charging a cent for postage, cost of drafts, or
time consumed in taking care of this phase of the work. . . . We,
therefore, urge upon our readers the necessity of laying aside
a portion for the missionaries each week, even but a ten-cent
piece . . . We will gladly forward, free, any sum whether it be
great or small."

And thus was established the policy of forwarding missionary
offerings 100% to the field, a policy to which the Assemblies
of God still adheres.[4]

The work rapidly outgrew the facilities at Findlay, and
a number of administrative problems needed action by the
entire organization. Therefore, since they were authorized
by the initial Council to call another Council when they
deemed it advisable, the Executive Presbyters announced
the second General Council for November 15-29, just seven
months after Hot Springs. The site chosen was the Stone
Church, then located on Indiana Avenue, in Chicago.

No attempt was made for quite a few years to record the
number of members in the affiliated assemblies. Undoubtedly, the number rose at approximately the same rate
as that of the ministers. One hundred and twenty-eight
preachers signed the roster at Hot Springs, and by the
close of the Chicago Council the ministerial list had grown
to five hundred and twenty-two, with thirty-five states,
Canada, and six foreign countries represented. The Assemblies of God was a growing movement simply because there
was no chance of any assembly losing its sovereign status,
while gaining the legitimate protection of a fellowship
which God had established for the good of His people.
There was nothing to lose, and everything to gain.

When the second Council was convened in Chicago,
Arch P. Collins was chosen to serve as Chairman and J. R.
Flower was re-elected to serve as Secretary. The Council
then took the step of electing D. C. O. Opperman as
Assistant Chairman and B. F. Lawrence as Assistant Secretary. The choice of these two officers was for this Council
only, and the choosing of assistant presiding officers was
not continued in succeeding Council until years later.

---

[4] *Early History of the Assemblies of God*, pp. 18, 19.

The form of organization adopted in the beginning was exceedingly simple. No headquarters had been authorized and none established. The nearest approach to a headquarters was the location of the publishing interests of the Council, and the fact that the first Chairman and Secretary served on the editorial staff of publications. When the second Council was convened, the presiding officer was elected for that meeting only. No duties were prescribed for him, beyond the simple duties of Chairman. Bell was retained as Editor of periodicals, and Flower as office editor.

The task of issuing credentials to qualified ministers was still allotted to H. A. Goss for the Western states and to T. K. Leonard for the Eastern states. It was not until the close of the 1916 Council that the issuing of ministerial credentials was assigned to the offices of the Chairman and Secretary, the publication offices by that time having reached the status of a headquarters for the fellowship.

The convention increased the original number of Executive Presbyters from twelve to sixteen, in order that the group might be more representative of the entire country. All of the incumbents were re-elected and five others were added: F. F. Bosworth, W. F. Carothers, George Chambers, Andrew L. Fraser, and David H. McDowell. The role of these presbyters was spelled out at this Council. They were to serve as advisers to the assemblies in their area; guides to the immature congregations, but with the ultimate goal always in mind—the recognition of such assemblies as self-governing; under no circumstances were they to intrude into the affairs of the sovereign assembly without an official invitation; local assemblies were expected to help to defray their guest's expenses.

Perhaps the most far-reaching decision of this Council was:

the Executive Presbytery is hereby authorized to take immediate steps in securing funds through voluntary offerings, subscriptions, or the sale of non-participating stocks, or in any manner pleasing to God and the Executive Presbytery of an amount not less than $5,000 for publishing equipment to be owned and controlled entirely by the General Council and to be used for the Glory of God.

Armed with this resolution and desiring to establish the
publication offices in a more central location, the brethren
moved the Gospel Publishing House in the spring of 1915
from Findlay to 2838 Easton Avenue, St. Louis, Missouri.
Since there was not a great deal of printing and office
equipment, the move was not too difficult.

An early model Huber press of sufficient capacity to
print four pages of newspaper size was donated by a
resident of Washington, D. C. It was originally bought to
do government printing, but it was now going to be active
in the King's business. A cutting machine was included in
the gift. A secondhand linotype machine and a secondhand
folding machine were also purchased. All the new equipment was installed in the storeroom on Easton Avenue,
after the floor had been reinforced to bear the weight
of the machinery. The second floor became the headquarters offices of the Assemblies of God.

Flower was to write of those days:

We had been authorized to establish a publishing house, but
nothing had been given us to accomplish our purpose. In those
early days, Brother Bell tried to live on $5.00 a week, which
he took out of the funds for support of himself and family.
Of course, he could not live on any such amount, and so he
ran behind in his finances continually. Then after the move to
St. Louis where increased rents were met and living expenses
were higher (especially during war times), he accepted the
munificent salary of $15.00 per week... Only the utmost frugality
could have brought into existence a publishing house under such
conditions. Such help as was required in the printing department
must be secured at small wages; and if we could do the work
ourselves the help had to be dispensed with. A visitor during
those days might have found Brother Bell bending over a piece
of machinery, with grease smeared on his shirt, his hands or his
face. He would straighten up, and although weary and worn, would
take the time to be courteous and kind.[5]

The sojourn in St. Louis was not to be lengthy; only
three years, in fact. But these were to be three of the
most fateful years in Assemblies of God history. Out on
the West Coast a small cloud had risen which was to develop
into the fiercest storm ever to be encountered by this
newly launched Pentecostal vessel.

---

[5] *Pentecostal Evangel*, June 30, 1923.

CHAPTER **6**

"THE NEW ISSUE"

A preacher who did not dig up some new slant on a Scripture, or get some new revelation to his own heart ever so often; a preacher who did not propagate it, defend it, and if necessary, be prepared to lay down his life for it, was considered slow, stupid, unspiritual ... Calling a man "a compromiser" killed his ministry far and wide. Because of this, no doubt, many new revelations began to cause confusion.[1]

California gave the Pentecostal Movement its greatest impetus in April, 1906, and just seven years later, in April, 1913, its sunny shores brought forth a "revelation" that almost tore the Movement apart. A Worldwide Pentecostal Camp Meeting, with Mary Woodworth Etter as the main speaker, was in progress in Arroyo Seco. Many miracles were wrought through the wonderful name of Jesus. One man, John G. Scheppe, was so inspired that he spent a night in prayer. Along toward morning he was given a glimpse of the power of that blessed name. Leaping to his feet, he ran through the camp, shouting to all the early risers what the Lord had shown him. The "revelation" made a profound impression upon the campers, and all rejoiced with Scheppe, and began to search the Scriptures concerning the "name of Jesus."

Unfortunately, that which should have been a most edifying study of the Word of God was diverted .by the enemy into a distressing error which almost ruined the work of God. Satan, realizing what a disaster would befall his kingdom if the people of God were really to grasp the power in the precious name of Jesus, adroitly maneuvered

---

[1] Goss, *op. cit.*, p. 155.

41

these sincere souls into heresy and fanaticism. His first tactic was to turn their eyes from Jesus Himself to a baptismal formula. True baptism, it was asserted, must be "in the name of Jesus," and not "in the name of the Father, and of the Son, and of the Holy Ghost." Some had used the shorter formula for years, so its use was no drastic innovation. What was new was the insistence that one *must* be thus baptized, in order to be "born of water." This created an immediate division among the saints on the West Coast. Frank Ewart, the editor of *Meat in Due Season,* and Glenn A. Cook, an Azusa Street veteran, were especially zealous in propagating the virtues of baptism with the single name formula, baptizing or rebaptizing all "according to Acts 2:38 and John 3:5."

"Baptismal regeneration" and unevangelical ritualism were but their first steps in the direction of heresy. To justify their "apostolic formula," Ewart, Cook, and company declared that a second "revelation" had been given them concerning the name: The reason why Peter did not use the longer formula of Matthew 28:19 was that the Spirit had revealed to him at Pentecost that "the name of the Father, and of the Son, and of the Holy Ghost is Jesus Christ!" Next came a denial of the Trinity. It was alleged that there were not three Persons in the Godhead, only three manifestations of one Person. Critics were told, "You must 'have the light' to see these marvelous truths." The capstone was a teaching designed to appeal to Pentecostal pride: "The baptism with the Spirit according to Acts 2:4 is what Jesus called being 'born of the Spirit,' and as such is necessary for salvation." [2]

The "New Issue," as it was labeled, was confined largely to the West Coast until January, 1915, when a tour by Cook brought this so-called "revelation" to St. Louis. The J. Roswell Flowers (already in the city in connection with the move of the General Council headquarters from Findlay) had known Cook since he had brought the Pentecostal message to Indianapolis in 1907. They listened with interest to his week of sermons in Mother Mary

[2] For a Trinitarian answer to the Oneness or "Jesus Only" doctrine concerning the Godhead and water baptism, see the author's *God in Three Persons.*

Barnes' Faith Home, and were onlookers when Mother Barnes and her staff were rebaptized in the waters of the Mississippi. Cook proclaimed that this baptism with its single name formula was, as in Gideon's day, "the water test." Only those who were alert, who were open to God's best, were going to pass the test.

But Flower did not accept this "revelation" from his old teacher. Instead, he wrote to G. T. Haywood in Indianapolis, warning him that Cook was on his way to that city with an erroneous doctrine. Haywood answered: "Your warning came too late. I have already accepted the message and been rebaptized." His church became a "Jesus Only" center, and continues to exert a strong Oneness influence even to this day. The wildfire that had been slow to start now began to leap from mission to mission, assembly to assembly, until it became *the* issue of the day.

It presented a major problem to the Assemblies of God leaders for the following reasons:

1. Any serious division would have been almost fatal to the not quite one-year-old organization.

2. A major plank in the Hot Springs platform was that there should be no theological creed to which all must subscribe.

3. No one had had time to produce an adequate answer to this Unitarian concept of the Godhead.

4. Many felt that the shorter baptismal formula was permissible.

The Oneness emphases upon the name of Jesus, the idea of a subjective "revelation," and the promise of additional power to all who accept the new message had a forceful appeal to Pentecostal believers, for they loved to exalt that name above all names, to receive truth experientially, and to keep being filled with the power of God.

Obviously, it became imperative that steps be taken to halt the spread of this extremism which was dividing the Movement. The editor of the *Weekly Evangel*, E. N. Bell, wrote an article for the March 27, 1915, issue, "Baptized Once for All," in which he remonstrated against this

rebaptism fad, pointing out that in the New Testament no
one who had received true Christian baptism was ever rebaptized. The April 17 issue carried an article on the Trinitarian view of the Godhead, written by D. W. Kerr. This was
followed by a series of editorials by Bell: "To Act in the
Name of Another" (May 1, 8); "The Great Outlook"
(May 29); "The Sad New Issue" (June 5); "The Acts
on Baptism in Christ's Name Only" (June 12); "Scriptural
Varieties in Baptismal Formula" (July 3). In all these
articles Bell emphasized the orthodox Trinitarian view of
the Godhead and defended the baptismal formula found
in Matthew 28:19.

The Executive Presbytery met in St. Louis in May, and
drew up a "Preliminary Statement Concerning the Principles Involved in the New Issue." Bell's explanation of the
statement, and the statement itself, appeared in the June,
1915, issue of the *Word and Witness*:

> For some months past this office has been besieged with
> inquiries concerning our attitude toward the so-called new doctrines,
> which are being preached in Los Angeles and some other places.
> One report came from the West Coast that it was being
> circulated in those regions that all the Presbyters of the General
> Council of the Assemblies of God had accepted these new
> doctrines, and we were asked if this were true. Both the
> Presbyters and this office, desiring more to preach Christ Himself
> and Him crucified and to promote love, peace and harmony
> among all of God's saints, have been loath to join horns in an
> issue over forms and ceremonies, which might lead to strife
> and division such as might cause us to lose sight of Christ
> Himself. We asked the people on the coast not to believe
> that the new teachers were responsible for these wrong reports,
> but to attribute them to false rumors. These reports and these
> inquiries, however, make it necessary for the Presbyters to set
> forth in some mild way, in love toward all, their attitude toward
> the more fundamental contentions in this new issue, as they
> have not the time to answer all these inquiries by private letter.
> Our brethren, too, have felt that we owed our readers a public
> statement on these issues. This office, not knowing the attitude
> of all these brethren, has not presumed to speak in their
> behalf, but has waited until the meeting of the Presbyters in St.
> Louis on May 11th, 1915, when after much prayer, deliberation
> and unity in the Spirit, it was deemed necessary to set forth
> the above Preliminary Statement.

The statement was as "mild" as the brethren could possibly make it, and Bell's explanation stressed that it was not to be considered "a creed, nor was it presented in a 'sectarian spirit,'" for it was a matter of "great regret" that the issue had to be discussed at all, since the new teachers held many truths in common with the brethren. But the statement was also as firm as the Presbyters could afford to make it at the time:

> We cannot accept a doctrine merely because someone claims to have a modern revelation to that effect ... such statements as, "the name of the Father, and of the Son, and of the Holy Ghost is Jesus Christ"; "that Christ is the Holy Ghost ..."

Other Oneness errors were also rejected in the statement. J. R. Flower, the General Secretary, spoke out personally in the columns of the *Word and Witness* on July 17, 1915. He had been studying the Bible and Church history for these months, and conversing with advocates and antagonists of the New Issue. Now, he felt, it would be criminal to keep silent any longer, for assemblies all over the country were being torn apart. The people of God must be awakened. Some had been swept off their feet, but were getting their bearings again. He was hopeful that in Los Angeles and St. Louis the crest of the wave had passed, echoing the sentiment voiced by Bell in the June 12 issue: "We venture to predict it is now at high watermark, and that the old issue so needless will dwindle down, as it always has."

But both Bell and Flower were too optimistic. A notice appeared in the same *Word and Witness* (July 17), advertising a camp meeting that was to be the scene of an event which was to send the New Issue sweeping to such heights that, for a time, the whole fellowship was in danger of being engulfed:

> The Third Interstate Encampment of the Assemblies of God, Jackson, Tenn., will begin July 23rd and continue to August 1st. We are looking to the Lord to send help of His own choice. This will be the largest and best attended camp ever held here, and we expect many to be saved and baptized and healed in Jesus' name ...
>
> H. G. RODGERS

Evangelist L. V. Roberts, of Indianapolis, one of the chief Oneness exponents, was startled to receive from this camp the following telegram signed by Rodgers *and E. N. Bell*: "We want your message for the camp. Take the first train."

After Roberts' first sermon, a shocked congregation heard Rodgers, the camp pastor, and Bell, the editor of the two official publications of the Assemblies of God, declare that they were candidates for baptism in Jesus' name! The next afternoon Bell was the first to be baptized, with scores of others following his example. The camp meeting mounted in enthusiasm, until on Sunday night there were approximately 4,000 people present. Roberts returned to his home via St. Louis, where he had the supreme joy of telling the thunderstruck Flower that he had been invited to the camp meeting in Jackson, Tennessee, and that he had just rebaptized Bell in Jesus' name.

One can well imagine the continent-wide consternation that greeted the news of Bell's defection. *Oneness* periodicals headlined his baptism, and it became a much-discussed topic of conversation in Pentecostal circles. Doubtless, some Assemblies of God men were wistfully thinking of former associations, where things might have been a little dead, but at least there had been no constant upheaval over wild doctrines. Did they long for the stability of the past?

Down in the Alto, Texas, camp meeting, William Burton McCafferty was instructing the saints against the errors of the New Issue. Harvey Shearer, the camp sponsor, rushed excitedly across the grounds one morning, waving a Oneness magazine, and shouting, "Read this!" Big, bold-faced type proclaimed: "E. N. BELL REBAPTIZED IN THE NAME OF JESUS!" "Now," Shearer exclaimed, "I suppose your tongue will cleave to the roof of your mouth."

"Why?" asked McCafferty.

"Well, when big men like E. N. Bell and L. C. Hall accept this teaching, little fellows like you and me had better keep quiet."

McCafferty's mouth set in a grim line. "I never was one to be stampeded into believing something that is not in the Bible. I don't care if the whole movement swallows this thing. I'm not going to, because it is wrong!"

Two of his coworkers at the camp were not quite as determined. Charles Smith, the evangelist, mused: "I wonder what L. C. Hall thinks about my salvation now. He baptized me 'in the name of the Father, and of the Son, and of the Holy Ghost.'" Smith added: "If Brother Mac here goes into it, I'll have to say it is in the Bible." But Smith did not wait for McCafferty to lead the way. L. C. Hall was conducting meetings in Caldwell, Texas, and succeeded in convincing Smith, who sent a card to McCafferty informing him he had been rebaptized by Hall. John Dye, another minister, indignantly told McCafferty: "If I take up with this New Issue, you can tell the world that I am crazy." He soon "took up" with it, but was not too happy later when McCafferty reminded him publicly of his statement.

A list of the "big men" who were being rebaptized, and accepting all or part of the Oneness belief about the Godhead, reads like the "Who's Who" of early-day Pentecost: E. N. Bell, Howard A. Goss, D. C. O. Opperman, L. C. Hall, G. T. Haywood, H. G. Rodgers, Glenn A. Cook, B. F. Lawrence, Harry Van Loon, and many other outstanding preachers, teachers, and writers. With rare exceptions, most of the Canadian brethren were included in this Oneness sweep. In Louisiana the Assemblies of God had twelve preachers: all twelve departed the Trinitarian faith. Where would this stop? It was becoming a veritable flood, and few had any hopes, or the ability, or the determination to halt it. There was a vacuum at the top, for Collins was not providing any decisive leadership.

One young man, not a "big man" in body but big in spirit and mind, dared to stand against the flood of false teaching. J. Roswell Flower was shaken by Bell's defection, but recovered enough to contact some of the Executive Presbyters and to gain their consent to call for a General Council in St. Louis in October. One must admire the courage and tact of this young man, for he was in an exceedingly delicate situation. The fate of the whole fellowship hung in the balance, and yet, a too drastic move against his chief could prove to be as damaging as the error that was deluging the Movement. Providentially for Flower and the Assemblies of God, he had a splendid helpmate whose prayer-saturated counsel at this time helped to steady him for the vital decisions which lay ahead.

In the same issue of the *Evangel* (August 14, 1915) in which Flower placed a call for a General Council, "to discuss and pray over certain problems now confronting the Assemblies of God," there appeared a provocative article submitted by Bell who had remained away from headquarters for several months. The title, "Who is Jesus Christ?" with its subheading, "Jesus Christ being rediscovered as the Jehovah of the Old Testament and the God of the New," was changed ("mutilated," according to Oneness adherents) by Flower with the substitution of "exalted" for "rediscovered."

The article itself, apart from the context of Bell's rebaptism and the controversy as a whole, was simply an exaltation of the Deity of Jesus Christ. It was Bell's stress upon Oneness proof texts, and his testimony concerning the ecstasy he felt as a result of the "revelation" he had received, that caused the article to be propagandized by anti-Trinitarians, and to be the source of dismay and bewilderment to those who had witnessed their champion desert to the opposition. What his friends on the Presbyter board wanted to know, and what the whole Movement wanted to know, was, "Why has this man so completely reversed his position?"

Bell sought to supply the answer in a later article (September 18, 1915), "There is Safety in Counsel," in which he appealed for all to come to the Council meeting. Nowhere was there the slightest repudiation of his action. On the contrary, he stated that he now saw that the apostles, in baptizing in Jesus' name, knew how to interpret Matthew 28:19! He explained that he felt the need of rebaptism after he was filled with the Spirit, but that he did not desire to bind any man's conscience, ride a hobby, or to condone the Oneness ideas about being "born of water and of the Spirit," or to join any faction.

His real reason slipped out—and it was not theological or ceremonial—he had found himself "in a corner." He felt dead in his soul. All his messages seemed taken away. Flower confirms this diagnosis. Bell had been working day and night, not only in his editorial duties, but also with the printing machinery. Such activity had made it almost impossible for him to pray as much as he desired, which, of course, contributed to his unsettled condition. At the camp meeting, Bell received an impression that, if he did not preach Acts 2:38, the camp would be the worst he had ever conducted. When he found the meetings were going flat, he obeyed the impression and sent the telegram to Roberts.

It is a sad mistake to abandon balance, just "to make the meeting go." And it is possible to be so active in exposing heresy, that in a weak moment one may become vulnerable to the heresy itself. "There are many voices," Paul says, and not all are from the Lord. One must try the spirits, and be especially careful when in a state of physical, mental, or emotional exhaustion. At such a time, the best safeguard is to accept only that which is fully and manifestly scriptural.

McCafferty almost succumbed in the same manner in Trenton, Missouri. He had been inveighing against the New Issue, when suddenly he felt strangely impelled toward it. He threw himself down before God. As far as he could see, the teaching was unscriptural, but it had a seductive appeal that almost ensnared him. McCafferty humbly confessed that he was but dust, that mightier men than he had fallen for this heresy. God gave him a word of comfort and strength: "A thousand shall fall at thy side, and ten thousand at thy right hand; but it shall not come nigh thee." [3]

Andrew F. Crouch was offered the assistant pastorate in a Pentecostal church in Winnipeg, pastored by Frank

---

[3] McCafferty, personal interview.

Small, a New Issue man. Crouch prayed earnestly to be
led by the Spirit into the truth. The answer meant a great
deal to this young preacher and his family, thousands of
miles from home, penniless and with no other calls. Not
only did security beckon, but he had to reckon with the
fact that many men in whom he had confidence had accepted this teaching. Yet, as he fasted and prayed, he saw
a vision of a gold chain with three links. The Spirit
impressed him with the truth that "the three links are one
chain but three *distinct* links." This Trinitarian belief cost
Crouch the position, but he had the satisfaction of em-
bracing a scriptural truth—and God supplied the material
need, too![4]

Meanwhile, in Puxico, Missouri, a convention was being
held which seemed ready to provide a major victory for the
Oneness forces. Despite the presence of Welch, some were
preaching the Oneness message and rebaptizing those who
accepted it. When this news reached Flower in St. Louis,
he persuaded a reluctant M. M. Pinson, who was passing
through the city, to hurry to Puxico. It was a sweltering
summer day. When Pinson walked into the church with
his two suitcases, his face was beet red and perspiration
dripped from his brow. E. N. Bell, who was in charge
of the service, said, "Brethren, I feel that Brother Pinson
has a word for us." A kindly soul brought a glass of water
to the platform, but Pinson (David-like) waved it away,
exclaiming, "Take that water away. That's *all* we've been
getting around here!" With that off his chest (but perhaps
still a little thirsty), Pinson preached a message on the
Trinity which helped to swing many back into line.

The 1915 General Council met in the Turner Hall, in St.
Louis, on October 1. The first three days were devoted
to testimonies, praise, and noncontroversial preaching. On
Sunday night there was a real move from God. This was in
keeping with the spirit of Hot Springs: first things first;
the Council is a fellowship, not a forum for debate; minds
may be divided, but hearts are one.[5]

---

[4] Mrs. A. F. Crouch, personal interview.
[5] Goss reported in the October, 1915, issue of the *Word and Witness* that at the
Arkansas State Camp Meeting "unity prevailed throughout the camp, even though
a great many preachers were there!"

Both the Chairman, A. P. Collins, and the Assistant Chairman, D. C. O. Opperman, failed to appear for the opening business meeting. Baptist Collins was not sympathetic with the idea of central authority, and by this time Opperman was well within the Oneness camp. Flower called the meeting to order, and J. W. Welch was asked to preside as Chairman pro tem and, later in the Council, was elected permanent Chairman. He was to serve in this post from 1915 to 1920. It was becoming increasingly evident that a strong, steadying hand was needed at the top. Welch was well-anchored in the Word, open for truth but conservative, fair but firm, and above all, filled with a spirit of good will and kindness to all. He was a gift from God "for such an hour as this."

Tuesday, October 5, was given over to the discussion of the baptismal formula. A spirit of brotherly love and courtesy marked the discussion. The selection of the speakers demonstrated the desire to hear both views: Bell and Haywood for Acts 2:38, and Collins and William G. Schell for Matthew 28:19. Schell removed himself when the discussion was limited to the Bible and his specialty, church history, was barred. Jacob ("Uncle Jake") Miller was appointed in his place. Schell was given his chance the next day, and waxed eloquent for two hours!

At the conclusion of the lengthy polemics, the Resolutions Committee offered a resolution pleading for a spirit of liberality to be applied to the question of the baptismal formula:

We strongly advise against all strife, harsh contention or division. . . . This Council refuses to attempt to bind the consciences of men in this matter, refuses to draw any line of Christian fellowship on either side of the question . . . so long as the person . . . keeps in a sweet Christian spirit, is not factious, does not tear up assemblies, etc.[6]

The general conviction prevailed that all should wait patiently for another year, allowing time for prayerful study of the Word, before reaching a definite conclusion.

Some doctrines were disapproved by a majority of the delegates:

---

[6] Minutes.

1. The use of fermented wine in the communion service [then being advocated by some ministers].

2. The confusing of the new birth with the Baptism or filling with the Spirit.

3. The failure to distinguish between the blood and the Holy Spirit.

4. The identification of the Father as the Son.

5. The identification of Christ as the Holy Ghost.[7]

That the tide was beginning to run against the Oneness views can be seen by the above resolutions. Bell resigned as editor, and Welch took over. No definitely committed Oneness man was placed on the Executive Presbytery. The *Evangel* report (November, 1915) proclaimed "Great Victory in Fellowship," apparently, because of the tolerance and patience manifested by both sides at the Council; but it was not a permanent peace, only an armed truce. The house was divided against itself, and no true peace could be possible until a basic agreement was reached on doctrinal beliefs. Still, with the Assemblies of God only 18 months old, even an uneasy peace seemed more desirable than open warfare. But while the *Weekly Evangel* was willing to let the issue slumber, its propagators were not, and the controversy broke out in increased fury.

Dire warnings were given to Trinitarians. Glenn A. Cook threatened Flower in St. Louis: "Roswell, if you fight against this Oneness message, this whole printing plant will be a pile of junk in six months." Howard Goss admonished E. L. Newby in Wichita Falls, Texas: "Be careful what you do about this wonderful truth. Don't turn it down finally, or you will miss God."

"But where is it in the Word?" inquired Newby.

"Oh, you'll never get this by studying it out like some other doctrine. This comes by 'revelation,'" replied Goss.

"Well, frankly, I'm not interested," declared Newby. "If you can't prove it in the Word, if it is not there plain and simple, I'd distrust any 'revelation' that communicated it. It's too farfetched for me."[8]

---

[7] *Ibid.*

[8] Newby, District Superintendent of Texas (1930-37), personal interview, Fort Worth, September 4, 1959.

This sentiment against the Oneness error began to crystal-lize in the hearts of many of the brethren from coast to coast. The truth about the Pentecostal Baptism had been so clear and so forceful in the Word that it would have required a "revelation" for them not to have seen it! But this new teaching was too dependent upon the subjective feelings of the individual, and in that realm it was easy for soulish mysticism to parade as spiritual revelation. The brethren could not build doctrines on fluctuating emotions. They needed a criterion that was constant: the unchange-able Word.

Also disturbing to many was the violation by New Issue men of a General Council policy (to which all had given consent), namely, that any man with a new teaching would not advance it until he was amid "a multitude of coun-sellors" where it could be threshed out. The purpose of this rule was to safeguard the Assemblies of God as a whole, but also to protect the individual himself from fol-lowing some impulse that might lead him into error and spiritual disaster. It was based upon a mutual confidence in each other's judgment. When A. P. Collins heard that Howard Goss had gone to Florida to preach the "Jesus Only" doctrine, he (at his own expense) followed Goss there, not to debate the question but to ask him to post-pone it until after the General Council. This great spirit of affection, this family tie, which made the brethren go to such great lengths to understand one another and to keep the peace, explains why the issue smouldered so long.

Nevertheless, a growing restlessness began to manifest itself among the Trinitarians. They wanted this issue set-tled once and for all: "How can the house stand, if it be divided on such basic doctrines? How can two walk together, except they be agreed? How can there continue to be a 'unity of the Spirit,' when there is no 'unity of the faith'?" This feeling communicated itself to headquarters, and at long last, J. W. Welch made this official pronouncement through the pages of the *Weekly Evangel* (June 24, 1916):

The coming Council will be what might be called an OPEN BIBLE COUNCIL. I think there is no doubt about that. It will be a Council in which the very most important questions

as to what the Bible teaches, will occupy the attention of all.
The time has come for the interpretation of what scriptural teaching
and conduct is. The time of sifting and solidifying is here. The
great shaking has begun, and all that can be disturbed will be
shaken into separation from that which is settled in God. This
will not all be done in a few days of Council, but lines will
doubtless be drawn ... It is time to take our bearings and to
assure ourselves before God.

Bethel Chapel, a small church in St. Louis, was the
meeting place of the Fourth General Council in October,
1916. This was to be the showdown. Tension was in the
air. Brethren who had labored closely together now found
that doctrinal disagreement brought a feeling of restraint.
The rival forces set themselves for the battle. This was
"the hour of decision."

A committee was appointed to prepare "a statement of
fundamental truths," and to bring the statement to the
floor. Named to the committee were T. K. Leonard, S. A.
Jamieson, D. W. Kerr, S. H. Frodsham,* and E. N. Bell.
It had been felt that, given time and fellowship, Bell would
reaffirm his belief in the Trinity and disclaim any connection with Oneness peculiarities of belief. This is pre-
cisely what happened. His temporary defection reminds
one of Peter's momentary lapse in Antioch, which caused
even Barnabas to be carried away with the dissimulation.
In all probability, Bell and others who had been influenced
by him to be rebaptized, but now with him were slowly
climbing back to solid theological ground, were to be
haunted through the years by his words in the June 12,
1915, *Weekly Evangel*: "I believe that every honest soul
who has done this [submitted to rebaptism] will one day
regret this step ... I can never go back on my Lord like
this!" Such words are reminiscent of the boast of the fish-

---

* At this Council J. W. Welch spoke to Mary A. Arthur, of Galena, Kansas,
"Sister Arthur, have you been praying, as I requested you to do, for God's
man as the Editor of the *Evangel*?" "Yes," she replied, "and every time I
pray the Lord shows me that the man who wrote this article is the one He has
chosen." She pointed to an article which had appeared in the Evangel of the
previous week, written by a young Englishman, Stanley Howard Frodsham. Welch
had already felt impressed that Frodsham was the man, and the words of
Sister Arthur, a woman of God in whom he had great confidence, confirmed it.
Frodsham served for the next five years as assistant editor, and then, with the
exception of a brief period in 1929, from 1921 to 1949 as Editor. He was also
elected as General Secretary in this 1916 Council and served until 1919.

erman apostle on another occasion. Nevertheless, as with his prototype, so with Bell, "the God of all grace" was able after he had suffered a while, to make him perfect, establish, strengthen, and settle him.

Each member of this wholly orthodox committee contributed his share, but the "statement of fundamental truths" was chiefly the work of one man, Daniel Warren Kerr, of Cleveland, Ohio. Kerr did not fit the popular conception of a powerful defender of the faith. A rather shy individual, a man of few words, seldom indulging in laughter, but able to light up the whole room with his smile. His dry wit was a help, too, in lightening the tension of debate and in taking the starch out of his opponents. He had done most of his work on this statement, before he came to Council.

Father Kerr was digging into the Word and reading Treffery on "The Eternal Sonship" for months, as well as every other old book he could find which had any bearing on the subject. We got it for breakfast, dinner and supper during those months! ... Never did I see him sit down for a few minutes that he did not pull out his Greek New Testament.[10]

At one time during these months of study of the nature of the Godhead, even former "CMA" Kerr wavered a bit toward the Oneness view. It should be realized there is a measure of truth in the emphasis upon the oneness of the Godhead, for "the Lord our God is one Lord." Anyone who delves deeply into theology must exercise great care to avoid the two extremes, absolute monotheism or equally false tritheism. It was providential that another former "CMA" man, David McDowell, came to Cleveland at this crucial hour, for it was his counsel that helped Kerr to regain his perspective. Out of this discussion and his own deep study, Kerr was able to prepare the copious notes that enabled the committee, in such a short time, to present a statement of truths that was both comprehensive and concise, and which today still forms a basic part of the doctrinal declarations of the Assemblies of God.[11]

---

[10] Willard C. Peirce, D. W. Kerr's son-in-law, letter to author, October 19, 1959.
[11] See Appendix.

Oneness men immediately questioned the right of the General Council to make such a statement: "Was it not declared in the formative Council at Hot Springs that the 'holy inspired Scriptures are the all-sufficient rule for faith and practice,' and we therefore shall not add to nor take from it? This statement represents a departure from the spirit of liberty and a return to the bondage of man-made creeds." However, the Trinitarians argued that the "Hot Springs Council declared that the fellowship had the right 'to disapprove of unscriptural methods, doctrines and conduct, and to approve all scriptural truth and conduct.' All that is being done on this occasion is to specify certain scriptural truths which are approved, and certain unscriptural doctrines which are disapproved, by the Assemblies of God."

Technically, both were correct, and both were wrong. This statement did represent a creed, but it was not necessarily opposed to the principles adopted at Hot Springs. The Oneness men had a Oneness policy for their periodicals; no Trinitarian doctrine would be allowed there, and no one could question the right of the editor to have a statement of faith for his publication. It was his sovereign right (even those who proclaim, "No creed but Christ," have a creed!). But this was an individual matter, whereas the Assemblies of God was a co-operative fellowship. True, but the fellowship had the right to state what it believed. It was a voluntary group: no one was coerced to join it; no one was forced to stay with it. Consequently, it, too, had some sovereign rights.

J. W. Welch explained:

Out of past experiences we have learned much about the ways and means of promoting Bible order and keeping unity. We all agree that to keep the unity of the Spirit is of first importance, but we are finding that it is not easy when our platform or plane of fellowship is so broad that they who seriously disagree in matters of doctrine have equal right and liberty to preach and teach in the same assembly. We still hold the necessity of having unity in the Spirit that we may come into the unity of the faith, but we see that diverse teachings and various explanations make for perplexity of mind and seemingly affect our keeping in the Spirit, often making it impossible to keep anything like unity.[12]

Also, there was a scriptural precedent for a statement of truths: the first General Council of the Early Church in Acts 15, and, for that matter, the entire New Testament. "Holy men of God" were simply transcribing what they had witnessed and experienced, writing the "apostles' doctrine," explaining what they believed. This was their prerogative and their duty. When erroneous doctrines threaten the purity of the faith, what can the Church do but draw up a doctrinal statement that pithily expresses the unsystematized scriptural truths, a statement which acts as a protecting wall around the sacred deposit of saving truth?

Creeds have their dangers. They become at times a strait jacket into which divine truth is squeezed; whereas, John Robinson, the spiritual guide to the Pilgrim Fathers, was right in saying: "There is more light to break from the old Book yet." Creeds can become substitutes for a real heart-experience. They are impersonal, while Christ Himself is intensely personal. Believing some hard and fast creed that contains only one phase of truth can hinder salvation (for example, hyper-Calvinism or hyper-Arminianism). Creeds have also made some to feel that any who differ with them are automatically outside of Christ.

Nevertheless, there is a genuine value in creeds.

Though the interpretation of Christianity contained in creeds is imperfect, sometimes inaccurate, sometimes one-sided, the creeds would not have arisen unless there had been someone and something to explain. Thanks be unto God that we know that Someone and possess that Something! As long as the Church has a Saviour to offer, it will find it necessary to explain who He is. As long as the Church has a real experience to offer to the world, it will need a form of words to describe it.[13]

The members of the Assemblies of God who had embraced the "Oneness" doctrine attended the fourth General Council with the hope, apparently, that there would be a swing from neutrality to a definite acceptance of the new teachings and practices. A group of them sat together,

---

and as the report of the committee was being considered, point by point, they voted solidly in opposition to adoption.

Following one negative vote, Chairman Welch leaned forward and expostulated with Howard Goss:

"Howard, you know you believe this point to be Gospel truth!"

"Sure I do," retorted Goss, "but you are making a creed, and I am opposed to it."

It was in the best interests of the "Jesus Only" group for the Assemblies of God not to adopt any theological statement, to enable them to retain membership and at the same time be free to propagate their new theology.

As the sections of the report on Fundamental Truths were considered, there was spirited and sometimes humorous debate. At one point, T. K. Leonard facetiously referred to the "Oneness" doctrine of G. T. Haywood and his colleagues as "hay, wood and stubble," with the further remark, "they are all in the wilderness and they have a voice in the wilderness," (referring to the periodical published by Brother Haywood entitled a *Voice in the Wilderness*). Haywood turned pale and started to rise to his feet, but was pulled back into his chair by those sitting near him. Ewart and Van Loon were not members, but they had not been denied the right to the floor. Gilbert Sweaza, a member from Southeast Missouri, red-faced and indignant, stomped out the door. Voices from both sides were raised in protest, and it was some minutes before things quieted down and the reading of the report was continued. From that time on, the advocates of the new doctrine took little part in the discussions, having come to the conclusion that opposition would be futile: the tide had definitely turned against them. The prophecy was made, however, that this action of the Council would split the Assemblies of God in two.

Yet, the discussion was marked by some highly edifying and instructive remarks. Mark Levy, a converted Jew, was given the privilege of the floor, and proved to be an able exponent of the Trinitarian doctrine, citing current Jewish worship and customs as illustrations: The worship-

ful echoing by Jews of the seraphim's "Holy, Holy, Holy";
the three unleavened cakes in the Passover meal, the middle
one alone being broken; the three strokes—one on each
doorpost and one on the lintel of each Hebrew home; the
two triangles in the shield of David, signifying the triune
nature of God and man. Levy also had a point about water
baptism: A Hebrew infant was circumcised on the eighth
day, not to make him a Hebrew, but because he was a
Hebrew. Similarly, a babe in Christ is baptized, not to
make him a Christian, but because he *is* a Christian.

One of the most extraordinary occurrences during the
discussion was the breath-taking moment when someone
began singing Reginald Heber's majestic hymn, "Holy,
Holy, Holy." As one man, the audience arose, and even
the anti-Trinitarians lifted up their hands in worship, and
sang, "God in three persons, blessed Trinity"! Surely, despite the turmoil and the sharply contrasting views concerning His nature, God Himself was in the place.

By the adoption of the statement of basic beliefs, this
1916 Council forced the Oneness adherents to propagate
their errors from outside the Assemblies of God. The list
of ordained ministers plummeted from 585 to 429, and the
total missionary giving shrank proportionately.

Those who would judge the Movement harshly for its
lack of stability in these formative days should reflect that
errors invaded even the New Testament churches, and that
for centuries the entire Church hovered between Trinitar-
ianism on the one hand and Sabellianism and Arianism on
the other. As a child explores his world, so these Pentecostal pioneers were exploring the world of theology. The
"old and cold" denominations had cast them out, making
them question the "old," and to be wide open for anything "new." Of necessity, there were "growing pains."
To reach maturity, they must learn to retain their child-
like faith in the supernatural leadings of the Holy Spirit,
without recklessly following every impression and suggestion. They must learn to read the Scriptures with eyes
not veiled by unscriptural traditions, and yet to "hold fast
that which is good" which they had received from the
fathers.

The important thing to remember is that, although this Sabellian heresy came within a hair's breadth of capturing the Assemblies of God, the two-year-old Movement did not succumb. By the grace of God, it survived the broiling heat of unresolved controversy and the thunderings and lightnings of all-out debate, and now was breathing deeply of the fresh, cool air of final decision. The storm was over, and the damage, while heavy—156 ministers and numerous assemblies missing—was not disastrous. Already the losses were being compensated, for many who had watched the fireworks from the sidelines began to write letters of congratulations and to inquire about membership. It was manifest that, at last, this newcomer to the church world was achieving a measure of that third factor of success—*stability*.

CHAPTER 7

"SALUBRIOUS SPRINGFIELD"

So here we are in salubrious Springfield right on top of the Ozark Mountains, out from the dirt and din of a great city, enjoying the pure air of a beautiful place that seems more like country than town, shouting the praises of God.[1]

The 1917 General Council had authorized the securing of better premises for the Gospel Publishing House. For several years the brethren had been trying to operate in "small, inconvenient, dingy, unhealthy quarters in one of the dirtiest parts of St. Louis, and many were the prayers that were breathed up to heaven for a more commodious and cleaner location."[2] The Lord spoke to the heart of one brother to loan $3,000 for this purpose, interest free, to be repaid in three $1,000 payments. An elderly lady offered $3,500 to be repaid at the rate of $60 per month until her death. A search was made in St. Louis, but no suitable property could be found for the money which the Council had to invest.

E. N. Bell was sent on a tour of a number of neighboring towns in Missouri and Iowa, and he returned to a special meeting of the Executive Presbytery with a good report. He had discovered an excellent buy in Springfield, Missouri, ideal premises for a printing plant and publishing house, and available for one-fourth of its value of $12,000. Flower was dispatched to the city known as the "Queen of the Ozarks," to confirm the report, and to pro-

---

[1] *Christian Evangel*, June 1, 1918. The periodical was known as the *Weekly Evangel* while published in St. Louis, but the title was changed back to *Christian Evangel* upon moving to Springfield. Later the name was changed again, this time to *The Pentecostal Evangel*.

[2] *Ibid.*

ceed with the purchase of the property. He was also asked
to relinquish his field ministry and to oversee the moving
and the setting up of the presses in the new building.

T. K. Leonard jokingly accused the brethren, who had
departed from his Findlay quarters three years previously,
of "fleeing into the wilderness," but the cloud of God's
presence was definitely leading into this Missouri "wilderness." Besides its "salubrious" qualities, there were other
good reasons for locating the Assemblies of God headquarters in Springfield. Real estate prices were much lower
than in the large cities; Springfield was the center of an
excellent rail system for the distribution of mail throughout
the country; its civic leaders were enthusiastically welcom-
ing the move, and even offering financial assistance. It is
doubtful whether better co-operation could have been ob-
tained from any other town or city in the whole United
States. The following typical editorial from a Springfield
newspaper indicates that the city feels that the relationship
has been mutually beneficial:

> The Assemblies of God is one of Springfield's greatest in-
> dustries—if you can call a church an industry—just as important
> to Springfield commercially as a great factory. It is an admirable
> industry—it creates no smoke or stench, it has no labor problems,
> it has no seasonal shutdowns, it never runs out of material
> and it never seems to have any difficulty meeting its payrolls.
>
> Its managers and employees, to continue to speak—not dis-
> respectfully, I hope—in industrial terms, are substantial and
> respectable citizens engaged in an enterprise which requires no
> apology and needs no federal subsidy or supervision. Its product
> is in constant demand and there is no evidence that its
> market will ever be exhausted.
>
> The moving picture theaters, the taprooms, the tobacco counters . . .
> may not profit extensively from the patronage of the Assemblies'
> staff and followers—but that is a situation which does not . . .
> bring tears to my eyes.
>
> As a non-participant in the activities of the Assemblies of God,
> but as an active well-wisher for the church's continued success
> and growth, I think that I am entitled to repeat that it is one
> of Springfield's most impressive and valuable assets and one
> which, I hope, will continue to make substantial inroads upon
> our news space.[3]

---

[3] *Springfield News Leader*, March 7, 1948.

The new Gospel Publishing House was a two-story 45 x 60-feet brick building (a former grocery and meat market) located at the corner of Lyon and Pacific Streets. The lower part consisted of two large rooms with concrete floor, which was ideal for the housing of the machinery and for the mailing of the paper. On the second floor there were nine large rooms for offices and a commodious hall. Growth in the fellowship has been reflected through the years by the expansion of this plant. Five additions have been made, but this has not sufficed, for the growth of the headquarters necessitated the erection of a new printing plant on Boonville Avenue. The offices have remained in the old building, but at the present time, a new commodious office building is under construction, also located on Boonville, and adjoining the printing plant. Yet, when the final move is made, there will probably be many misty-eyed souls who will lift their hearts in gratitude for the old brick building on Pacific Street which has been "home" for so many years.[4]

A local assembly was to profit by the establishment of headquarters at Springfield. The congregation had been meeting in a rough, wooden tabernacle on East Central Street, but with the addition of new members, a lot was purchased at Campbell and Calhoun Streets as a site for a permanent edifice. Fred Vogler, who was pastoring a small church in Kansas, was asked to supervise the construction of this 40 x 60-foot building, which was completed in 1920. It, too, has known constant additions, until the ministry of James Van Meter (1954-1959) who led the church, which had become known as the Central Assembly, in the erection of a truly magnificent edifice on Boonville and Calhoun.

The growth in the fellowship, as a whole, was a big factor in the transfer of the headquarters to Springfield. After the drop from 585 to 429, as a result of the withdrawal of the Oneness dissenters, the number picked up until at the time of the 1917 Council in St. Louis it was 573, and by the 1918 Council, 728 ministers and 91 missionaries. Giving to the missionary cause in 1916 had amounted only to $4,879.50, but by 1917 it was up to $10,223.98, and by 1918 it had soared to $29,630.51. Mem-

---

[4] A 6-story International Distribution Center was added in 1971. The building also houses the Assemblies of God Graduate School.

bership in the local assemblies was steadily increasing, too. A businessman in Goose Creek (now Baytown), Texas, exclaimed to F. D. Davis, a newly ordained Assemblies of God evangelist, "You know, preacher, we used to be able to count Pentecostal people on our fingers, but now we have to count them by acres!"

But was it simply a real estate bargain, a hearty civic welcome, a healthful climate, a growing constituency, and a mid-continent location that brought the Assemblies of God to Springfield? In 1926 an elderly Pentecostal woman, Miss Alice A. E. Benedict, passed away in Aurora, Missouri, and her body was brought to the assembly in Springfield, where an impressive funeral service was held. A long-time resident of the city arose and told of the early days of the outpouring of the Holy Spirit in a tent which stood on the site now occupied by the assembly:

> There were only a handful of saints, but oh, how they prayed! Sister Benedict was under a tremendous burden night and day. The Lord had put it on her heart to pray for mighty things for Springfield, that God would make it a center from which His blessings would radiate to the ends of the earth. I believe this assembly, the Gospel Publishing House and Central Bible Institute are all here as a result of that "praying in the Holy Ghost" by Sister Benedict. [5]

When we add to this incident the vision given to Rachel Sizelove in 1913 [6] of "a beautiful, bubbling, sparkling fountain in the heart of the city of Springfield, which sprang up gradually but irresistibly, and began to flow toward the East and the West, the North and the South, until the whole land was deluged with water" we must conclude that it was *God* who led the brethren to Springfield, and "all these things" were added for good measure.

Immediately following the move to Springfield, the decision was made to hold the Sixth General Council in that city. This would give the delegates an opportunity to inspect the new premises, and it would be helpful for the city to see a representation of Assemblies of God men

---

[5] Reported in the *Pentecostal Evangel*, April 9, 1927.
[6] See Chapter 7, *A Sound from Heaven*, Carl Brumback (Springfield, Mo: Gospel Publishing House, 1977).

and women from all over the country. The old Diemer
Theater on Commercial Street was chosen as the auditorium
in which to hold the convention. J. Roswell Flower re-
members it well, for he washed the chairs and mopped
the floor in preparation for the Council! It was a Council
for all to remember, for here the distinctive testimony of
the Assemblies of God was subjected to its sternest test.

CHAPTER **8**

"DO ALL SPEAK WITH TONGUES?"

It is with regret that I return my credentials, but I believe that it is the consistent thing to do, since I do not believe, nor can I ever teach, that all will speak in tongues when baptized in the Spirit . . . I pray that at the next Council the subject of the Bible evidence will be lovingly considered from the Scriptures.[1]

These words touched a nerve center—the distinctive teaching of the Pentecostal Movement, viz., that speaking with other tongues always accompanies the Baptism or infilling with the Holy Spirit. It was the reason for separate existence, the point of divergence with other evangelicals who believed in an infilling subsequent to conversion. It was the belief that marked one, doctrinally, as Pentecostal.

Although this teaching had often been attacked by non-Pentecostalists, only once before had it been brought under fire by those within the Movement itself. A convention and short-term Bible school was conducted in Waco, Texas, in February, 1907, for the purpose of giving a fair and open discussion of points of doctrine. New ministers in the Movement were raising questions in regard to a number of Pentecostal teachings, particularly tongues as the initial, physical evidence of the baptism in the Spirit. A. G. Canada and his group contended that any one of the gifts could be the immediate, outward manifestation of the experience, but W. F. Carrothers argued so conclusively for the orthodox Pentecostal position that the question was settled for most of those present once and for all.

It was decided that San Antonio, the next city slated to receive the Pentecostal message, was to be a test case. The

---

[1] Letter from F. F. Bosworth to J. W. Welch, July 24, 1918.

brethren covenanted together not to mention anything about evidential tongues. No one else had taught the doctrine there, and it was felt that, for the sake of those whose arguments had been defeated in Waco, it would be good simply to commit the results to the Lord. Consequently, no seeker was expecting tongues, but, as at Jerusalem, so at San Antonio, "all . . . began to speak in other tongues as the Spirit gave them utterance!" D. C. O. Opperman and L. C. Hall were among those filled at this meeting. This early-day confirmation helped to establish the doctrine as a permanent tenet in the Pentecostal Movement.

But now, eleven years later, the question was being raised again, and this time it was not by a newcomer, but by a Pentecostal veteran, one of the finest men ever to grace the Movement, F. F. Bosworth. As a young man in Zion City, Illinois, he had witnessed Marie Burgess (later Mrs. Robert Brown) receive such a remarkable infilling that he himself became so hungry that he, too, received that same night. The hand of God was upon him from the first. Bosworth was a sweet-spirited man, an avid student of the Scriptures, an eloquent speaker, and his healing ministry was outstanding. He had suffered for his Pentecostal testimony, and once was so destitute that he had been forced to gather gleanings from grain cars for food, and once was taken by a mob and tarred and feathered. His tremendous success in the Dallas area had made it a prominent Pentecostal center, and the revivals at his Dallas church were regarded as "great revivals" in the days when revivals were *revivals!*

Bosworth had been one of the 120 delegates at the Hot Springs Council, and had served as an executive presbyter in the Assemblies of God, signifying that he was in complete agreement with the doctrinal position of the fellowship. But somewhere along the line, doubts began to creep into Bosworth's mind concerning "evidential tongues." His study of the lives and ministries of great men of God who had not spoken in tongues made him wonder about the correctness of the Pentecostal position. The shallow experi-

ence of some Pentecostal people seems to have been the
major stumbling block, too.

According to several men who were acquainted with
Bosworth's Pentecostal ministry, he had adopted a mechan-
istic method in his dealing with candidates for the infilling with the Spirit. He emphasized the need of faith
for an immediate reception: "There is no longer any need
to tarry in the dispensational sense of the early disciples.
The fact that, even in the case of the disciples at Pentecost, '*they* (not the Spirit) began to speak in other tongues,'
means that one must speak forth in faith." There was an
element of truth in this emphasis, and it proved to be
just what some timid, fearful souls needed. They had surrendered all but the physical, and this word helped them
to yield their bodies as temples of the Holy Ghost.

On the other hand, there were candidates who had not
yielded, who were not ready, and his stress upon the experience as "a gift, nothing to give up, no need to tarry,
just speak out in faith," wrought disaster in their lives.
They received nothing but a psychic experience, which
created doubt in their own minds about the validity of
the Baptism, and added nothing at all to their lives. What
Bosworth overlooked in his emphasis upon the individual's
faith in the matter of speaking in tongues was that Acts
2:4 tells us that *something else occurred before* "they began
to speak in other tongues": "they were all *filled* with the
Holy Ghost"! The supernatural filling preceded the supernatural speaking: the filling was the cause, not the
effect. Furthermore, the mighty infilling with the Spirit
which thousands of Pentecostalists had experienced had
reached the inner depths, because, while a gift unmerited,
it had been preceded by much soul-searching and consecration. There is no shortcut to a real experience: *spiritual*
power can never come through the employment of a physical or psychical technique. True Pentecostalists are not interested in how many noses (or tongues) they can count
as "Baptism statistics," but are vitally concerned that all
receive a genuine New Testament experience that revolu-
tionizes the life of the believer and adds to the total power
of the Church.

When Bosworth saw the result of his emphasis, he was as dismayed as Luther when the latter witnessed the licentiousness that some of his followers mistook for liberty. But unlike Luther, who did not renounce his basic teaching of salvation through grace because of the extremes which resulted from it, Bosworth began to question the basic teaching of tongues as the constant accompaniment of the baptism with the Spirit. What he should have questioned was his emphasis upon the human element in this glossolalic experience, and then returned to the divine emphasis of his early days in Pentecost. As this report from Plymouth, Indiana, to the *Latter Rain Evangel* (December, 1908) makes clear, Bosworth once believed that tongues was the evidence:

We have never taught the people to expect anything more than the glory and power of the Lord and the "unknown tongue" to accompany the immersing in the Holy Spirit, so there has never been the slightest tendency toward fanaticism or extremes from the beginning, and nothing has occurred that has not been edifying ... God's hungry ones are being baptized in the Holy Spirit in accordance with Acts 2:4 ... One night a few weeks ago, while the people were standing for dismissal, God pressed me to urge them to much closet prayer, and while I was speaking, His Spirit fell on me in greater power than I had ever before experienced, and spoke in a loud voice in another language, which He interpreted through one of the other workers. While the Spirit yet spake through me, the power of God fell upon a sister from La Paz, exactly as He did upon the household of Cornelius, Acts 10:44-46. Instantly she began to address the audience with a loud voice, speaking a beautiful message which was also interpreted by the sister on the platform. We knew God had baptized her, "for we all heard her speak in tongues and magnify God."

The pendulum swung for Bosworth away from *his* unwise methods to his adoption of the belief that the *glossolalia* is but one of the gifts that a sovereign God may bestow upon recipients of the Spirit. It was *one* evidence, he asserted, but not the only one, and it was "revolting to judge a person's experience solely by whether or not he had spoken in tongues." Of course, this was a caricature of the Pentecostal belief. Like Paul, the Movement did not esteem tongues as the sum and substance of all experience or conduct. An enduement of power which would enable the recipient to worship supernaturally, to witness effectively, to walk in the Spirit, and to love souls—this was the goal held out to candidates for the baptism in the Spirit.

Nevertheless, Bosworth began to express his views that speaking in tongues is "one evidence, but only one—there are many other outward signs of the inward filling, and this particular gift should not be required in every instance." He was a persuasive man, and a good man in whom a great many Pentecostalists had a great deal of confidence. Three of his close friends, men with wide influence in the Assemblies of God, W. T. Gaston, M. M. Pinson, and A. P. Collins, were swayed by his arguments. Emboldened, Bosworth began to introduce his views into his sermons.

Letters began to arrive at headquarters, protesting these non-Pentecostal ideas. The executive brethren were reluctant to initiate any kind of action against so exemplary a man as Bosworth. They admired him tremendously, but apart from their own admiration and affection for him, they hoped that his views might swing back to the Pentecostal position. Still, there was enough agitation that in the 1917 Council in St. Louis a resolution was adopted to the effect that only missionaries who subscribed to the Assemblies of God statement of fundamental truths could from henceforth receive credentials. The reason given for the resolution was that some were calling into question the doctrine of evidential tongues.

It was felt that a few articles in the *Christian Evangel* might help, so messages on the baptism in the Spirit by W. H. Pope, William Durham, W. Jethro Walthall, and D. W. Kerr appeared during the summer of 1918. In the July 27 issue, hope was expressed that "doctrine will not be the major discussion at this Council as at the last two ... we trust that we have settled our Fundamental truths." But by the August 24th issue, it was conceded that all the major doctrines held by the Assemblies of God would be discussed at the coming Council. It was not known just how many had been infected by the non-Pentecostal opinions.

Meanwhile, on July 24, at his home in Dallas, F. F. Bosworth sat down at his typewriter and began writing the letter, an excerpt from which began this chapter. He speaks of receiving "a couple of letters from the brethren telling me I had no right to hold credentials, so I believe it is best to return them. They will blame you if I hold on to them and you don't call them in." Nevertheless, Bosworth decided to attend the Council in Springfield, where he hoped "the subject of the Bible evidence will be lovingly considered."

The subject was considered in a spirit of love, apparently, even though the debaters grew rather vehement on that Saturday afternoon, September 7, in the Diemer Theater. Joseph Tunmore had jumped the gun in the morning session, by speaking pointedly about tongues as the evidence, but the afternoon session "was taken up with an animated discussion on the importance of a united stand concerning the evidence." [2] Robert Brown, Joseph Tunmore, J. T. Boddy, T. K. Leonard, W. H. Pope, J. Rosselli, and others spoke vigorously in defense of this distinctive Pentecostal belief. "Utmost enthusiasm" was created by their sermonettes.

W. T. Gaston occasioned some dismay by asking for an explanation of the difference between the "gift" and the "evidence." Some thought by this request that he had completely accepted Bosworth's view (later incorporated in a tract, "Do All Speak with Tongues?"). Gaston had not, in fact, totally capitulated; all he wanted was a clarification of this vital point in the tongues question. [3] When M. M. Pinson, the doughty fighter, championed the "only one of the evidences" theory, the debate began to wax Sinaitic—hotter and louder! "Dear old Brother Collins, of Fort Worth, constantly brought the matter to a more peaceable vein with his fatherly and spiritual admonitions." [4] Though no longer a member, Bosworth was extended the courtesy of the floor. He did not attempt to press his views

---

[2] *Minutes.*

[3] For a full explanation of the differences between the two aspects of tongues, see the author's book *What Meaneth This?*

[4] Personal letter to author from W. J. Kirkpatrick.

upon the Council, but it was clear that he fully believed
what he had written in his letter: "If I had a thousand
souls, I would not be afraid to risk them all on the truth
of my position that some may receive the fullest baptism
in the Spirit without receiving the gift of tongues."

Even the most rabid Pentecostalists could assure Bosworth
that he need not risk the one soul he did have on such
a proposition, for they fully agreed that the "gift of tongues"
is not given to all, but they did contend that the "gift"
was not the same in purpose and operation as the speaking in tongues that occurs at the baptism in the Holy Spirit.
As for the experiences of great men who had not spoken in
tongues, T. K. Leonard advised Bosworth: "I would spend
more time in getting an experience that fits the Bible
than I would in endeavoring to get the Bible to fit an
experience." [5] W. B. McCafferty, replying to Bosworth's
reference to Finney, called his attention to the fact that

Finney may have spoken in tongues, when he "literally bellowed
out the unutterable gushings" of his heart. Be that as it may,
the whole question is a matter of capacity. Finney was a barrel,
while most of us are a tumbler. Even if the barrel were only
half-full, it would still have more water in it than a mere glass that
was brim full. [6]

But it remained for D. W. Kerr, who had turned the
tide in the 1916 Council against the Oneness doctrine, to
bring the decisive answers to the questions raised on this
occasion. Kerr not only marshalled all the truths presented
by his brethren, but also drove home again and again that
it is the Word of God, not the experiences of famous
men, that is the touchstone for the Pentecostal belief concerning the immediate, outward evidence of the Baptism.
The Scriptural record had not been twisted by Pentecostalists; no isolated case had been set forth as the sole basis
for their belief; but in every case in which the results
of the experience in Acts are recorded, each recipient spoke
in tongues. Kerr also succeeded in answering conclusively
Gaston's query about the difference between the evidence

[5]*Christian Evangel*, October 5, 1918.
[6] *Ibid.*

and the gift. The *Minutes* tell us that "he set everybody to shouting."

W. T. Gaston, his heart yearning for his friend Bosworth, and with no desire to leave him alone, had been listening intently to Kerr's treatment of the subject. Point by point, truth upon truth, the argument had mounted until his doubts were swept away. The *Evangel* may have been describing him in these words: "One who had been somewhat hesitating said, in the words of a judge who had all the evidence brought to him on the same subject, 'It is enough!' " Gaston was later to pen an excellent tract on the difference between the evidence and the gift.

A strong resolution was presented at the close of Kerr's exposition; strong, but after all, the only logical position for a Pentecostal group to take:

Resolved, That this Council considers it a serious disagreement with the Fundamentals for any minister among us to teach contrary to our distinctive testimony that the baptism in the Holy Ghost is regularly accompanied by the initial, physical sign of speaking in other tongues, as the Spirit of God gives utterance, and that we consider it inconsistent and unscriptural for any minister to hold credentials with us who thus attacks as error our distinctive testimony.[7]

Of course, the resolution carried unanimously. Even Bosworth cast an unofficial vote in the affirmative, saying, "Well, I just voted myself out of the Assemblies of God."

The Assemblies of God lost a good man when F. F. Bosworth shook hands with his many friends and departed on the next train for the Christian and Missionary Alliance annual conference. He continued to be signally used of God in the ministry of evangelism and divine healing.[8] Theoretically, he also continued to believe in tongues as one of the evidences, but like so many who take this position, he feared to permit any form of tongues at all in his meetings—among seekers or elsewhere, for tongues would identify him anew with Pentecostalism. It would

---

[7] *Minutes.*

[8] A considerable number of the author's relatives were led to the Lord through miraculous healings which several of them received in Bosworth's 1927 campaign in Washington, D. C.

appear that, generally speaking, unless one is Pentecostal in his belief concerning speaking in tongues as the evidence, i.e., that *all* will speak in tongues at the infilling of the Spirit, he does not genuinely believe in tongues at all. In practice, either *all* speak, or *none* speak. If this be not a fair statement of the facts, let those who profess to believe that tongues is "one of the evidences" preach it *positively*, and encourage it whenever God begins to bestow this "gift" upon a seeker.

It is futile to speculate, but one cannot help wondering what would have happened if F. F. Bosworth had continued through the years to minister within Pentecostal ranks. Late in life, he was closely associated with Pentecostal men in healing campaigns so, in a sense, he fulfilled the desire of Stanley Frodsham, writing in the *Christian Evangel* (October 5, 1918) immediately after this Council: "We trust that we shall yet see them back taking their stand with us." A. P. Collins renewed his allegiance to the Pentecostal testimony, after hearing the discussion, and seeing the cloud of glory that rested upon the Council in apparent vindication of the truth. M. M. Pinson soon made a statement in the *Christian Evangel* (March 22, 1919) that Kerr's discourse and the statement in the Minutes had "cleared my mind on the tongues question."

On Tuesday morning, September 10, the following resolution was passed:

Whereas our distinctive testimony, expressed in the Fundamentals as to the speaking in tongues as the Spirit gives utterance being the sign of the baptism with the Spirit, has recently been called into question and characterized as error, therefore be it Resolved, That we hereby most heartily reassert our position on all the Fundamentals and especially on the point that speaking in tongues as the Spirit of God gives utterance is the initial, physical sign of the full consummation of the baptism with the Holy Spirit . . .[9]

This was one of the most vital Councils in the entire history of the Assemblies of God. The point of contention was not a peculiar bit of denominational dogma which the organization needed to justify its separate existence,

---

[9] *Minutes.*

but it was a contending for the faith in, and the experience of, the Spirit fullness of New Testament Christianity. One lesson learned was that the testimony is greater than any man. In a way, what a man believes is more important than what a man is. He may be sincere, kind, intellectual and a man of character, but if his beliefs are not according "to the law and to the testimony," he can be more dangerous than a person who has few of these good qualities. Sincerity must be accompanied by truth, and sweetness by light.

One further resolution at the 1918 Council demonstrated the fact that the Assemblies of God was not "against" anyone simply because he might not agree with the distinctive testimony: "Resolved, That we again declare our Christian fellowship with every true child of God, and that we stand ready to cooperate with all Christians. . . ." This resolution manifested a spirit of Christian love that extended beyond Pentecostal doctrine, but it also took a firm stand for what was believed to be the clear teaching of the Word of God. As a direct result of this Council, it was decided at the next General Council to change the name of the official organ from *The Christian Evangel* to *The Pentecostal Evangel;* not because the Assemblies of God desired to be less Christian, but rather, because the Assemblies of God desired to be more New Testament Christian.

CHAPTER **9**

"APPROVED UNTO GOD"

BIBLE SCHOOLS were destined to play a major role in the Assemblies of God. The twentieth-century outpouring of the Spirit began at Bethel Bible College in Topeka and gained a mighty impetus by the Pentecostal revival in Nyack Missionary Training Institute on the banks of the Hudson.

Short-term schools, such as the one announced to begin on December 6, 1915, at Hartford, Alabama, conferred a meager training upon the early preachers of the Movement:

> There will be a brief course in Bible history, a study of the special truths for this day and age in the form of topics . . . training in vocal music and grammar . . . evangelistic services every night . . . We propose to include much prayer and waiting on God for a special enduement of power from on high and gifts of the Spirit according to His own will . . . Each student is requested to bring his own toilet outfit, blankets, pillow, a hundred-fold consecration and a teachable spirit. Beside this, bring all the food and money God will give you.[1]

It soon became apparent that permanent schools would have to be established, with a curriculum modeled upon those of Nyack and Moody. Some opposition was voiced against this more formal type of training, because there were those who felt that it represented a step toward formality, a step toward the mind of man and away from the mind of the Holy Spirit. Bible school proponents replied that the mind of the Spirit was expressed in the

---

[1] *The Weekly Evangel*, December 4. 1915.

command which He had inspired: "Study to show thyself approved unto God, a workman that needeth not to be ashamed, rightly dividing the word of truth." [2] Only a diligent study of the Word could place in the mind that which the Spirit could bring to remembrance. The school of the prophets established by Samuel and the "school" of the disciples that was taught daily for at least three years by the Master Teacher should be regarded as abundant precedent. Furthermore, had not some of the most anointed Pentecostal men been trained at Nyack and Moody?

The Bible institutes were to be Bible-centered, concerned with a study *of* the Bible rather than a study *about* the Bible. The spiritual life of the students was to be the prime consideration, for it was vital that truth be translated into life. Evangelism and missions were to be emphasized, and thus much attention would be focused upon practical training. The great need was to equip the candidates with a fundamental knowledge of the Word and to send them forth quickly into the harvest field. Alice Reynolds Flower's hymn put into words the response of many Pentecostal young people to this need:

> Have I forgotten the call of the Master?
> Have I forgotten that sweet, sacred day,
> When to His pleading I gladly made answer,
> "Here, Lord, am I, send even me"?
>
> Have I forgotten that Jesus is coming?
> Have I forgotten my part in it all?
> Lord, help Thy servant to fail Thee no longer,
> Though it is late, I go at Thy call!

A resolution at the First General Council called attention to the Gospel School directed by T. K. Leonard in Findlay, Ohio. This school was to merge in 1917 with the Mount Tabor Bible School in Chicago, Illinois, conducted by Andrew Fraser, pastor of Bethel Temple. Another Chicago school, Ebenezer Bible Institute, under the leadership of David Wesley Myland, was an eighteen-week school with evening classes open to the public and with enrollment in

---

[2] 2 Timothy 2:15.

the day classes possible at any time.[3] Myland was a gifted singer, a member of the famous CMA Ohio quartet, and the writer of a number of spiritual hymns and songs. He was also the author of several books including a splendid book entitled *The Latter Rain Pentecost.*

GIBEAH

The Gibeah Bible School, in Plainfield, Indiana, was an earlier endeavor (1912-1914) by Myland and the J. R. Flowers:

The Flem Van Meters from Jasonville, Fred and Maggie Vogler from Zion City, Richard H. Gardiner and Eleanor Palmer from Chicago joined with us in every effort to develop this much needed center of solid, timely Bible teaching. Mr. Flower and I lived in a little cottage belonging to my father nearby, but we attended all the classes possible, and even today we are passing along vital truths quickened to our hearts by the Holy Spirit in those never-to-be-forgotten hours.

The attendance was never large, but the lessons were deep and sound. Brother Myland, a prince among Bible teachers, allowed some startling interruptions by the Holy Spirit to confirm the truths opened to the students. Sometimes the hush of God literally enfolded us as some special word dropped to our souls' very depth . . . There was a time in a class in Angelology when we were considering the three heavenly visitors who came to Abraham's tent door; and suddenly, it seemed that the swift brush of angel wings was in our midst. The remembrance of that holy hour before God brings the quick rush of tears to my eyes. We need more of such sacred moments in the study of God's Word, whether in private or class sessions. "The letter killeth"—but how unspeakably alive the Holy Ghost can make every searching and inspiring truth of our Lord.[4]

ELIM

The Rochester Bible Training School, operated in conjunction with the Elim Faith Home in Rochester, New York, was founded in 1895 by the five daughters of James Duncan, a Methodist pastor for more than twenty years. Mrs. E. V. Baker, the eldest daughter, acted as superin-

---

[3] An outstanding graduate of this school was John "Knox" Kellner, who, together with his wife, Olive, had an eminently successful ministry for 29 years in Binghamton, New York.

[4] Mrs. J. R. Flower, *Bread of Life*, a monthly magazine, Brooklyn, N. Y.

tendent, aided by her sisters, Mrs. M. E. Work, Mrs. N. A. Fell, Miss S. A. Duncan, and Miss H. M. Duncan.

Elim, as it was commonly called, was the first permanent school to make a genuine impression upon the Movement. A deep appreciation of the Word of God was inculcated in the hearts of the students. Living by faith was also stressed, and many chronicles might have been written concerning the supplying of material and physical needs. Crucifixion of the self-life was emphasized to such an extent that it apparently was permitted to exclude a commensurate emphasis upon the resurrected life. Works of evangelism were also neglected, with the explanation that "servants work, but sons worship." Notwithstanding the introspective and one-sided nature of the teaching, the classroom and chapel sessions were marked by depth and power.

Enrollment at Elim was never more than forty, but a startling proportion of the students achieved distinction in the Assemblies of God. Five alumni—Ralph M. Riggs, Gayle F. Lewis, Charles W. H. Scott,[5] Wilfred A. Brown, and Noel Perkin (a student-teacher)—were resident executive presbyters at one time. J. Z. Kamerer, General Manager of the Gospel Publishing House (1927-1952), is another prominent alumnus. Outstanding missionaries from the school include Harry Waggoner, Jacob Mueller, Mrs. Nicholas Nikoloff, and Elsie Blattner.

John Wright Follette was a youthful instructor at Elim. Scholar, poet, author, singer, musician, this Pentecostal descendant of Hugenot forebears was to spend many fruitful years ministering in Assemblies of God schools, churches, and conferences at home and abroad. On several occasions at Elim, Follette was given an exceptional manifestation of tongues. A Parisian linguist described one miracle of utterance as "impossible to an American, the intonation and variety of expression so unique, that it could not be

---

[5] Scott, reluctant to enter the ministry, was still in his home church in Montreal in 1922. Playing his xylophone one evening, he yawned, causing his jaw to lock in an awkward and painful position. Prayer to the Great Physician did not avail, and no other physician was available. Accepting the admonition of a brother, Scott surrendered his future to the Lord. Immediately, his jaw snapped shut! Even the pet canary blended his melodious trills with the praises that burst forth from the no-longer-reluctant Scott and his Canadian friends.

reproduced except in this supernatural manner." [6] There can be little doubt that the students, while not fully sharing all of Follette's enthusiastic iconoclasm, were sharpened by their contact with this brilliant and dedicated teacher.

The depth of the teaching was reflected in the depth of the Spirit's work among the students. At times, the whole congregation became a choir. The raw, untrained voices were transformed into a superb choral group, with a finesse, range of voice, and antiphonal effects that come only as a result of years of expert tutelage. On one occasion, a Dr. Carl Wittich, a German music professor whose brother became a pastor of the Stone Church in Chicago, came into the auditorium. Listening to the glorious tones and subtle shadings, all as if under the direction of a master chorister, Dr. Wittich became so conscious of the supernatural presence of God that he was converted on the spot, and later entered the Pentecostal ministry.

At a Sunday afternoon service two students, Jacob Mueller and John Allison, were asked to sing a duet. Both consented to sing, even though they felt unworthy, not yet having received the Spirit's fullness—a crime in those days! When their voices were lifted in song, a strange and incredible thing happened: the duet became a trio. A third voice, singing a high obbligato, could be heard distinctly by everyone in the room. For a few moments all sought to discover the identity of the third vocalist, looking first at the organist, then at the leader of the service, but each signalled that the voice came from some other source. When all possible suspects were eliminated and the vastly superior quality of the voice was recognized, it dawned upon all that, although their eyes were veiled, they were in the presence of a heavenly being. Like the men on the Damascus Road, they were amazed, "hearing a voice, but seeing no man."

Out of deference to this wondrous manifestation of the Spirit, but with no thought of its being repeated, the two young men were asked to sing on the following Sunday afternoon. Again, the duet became a trio—the same heav-

---

[6] Letter from Hattie Duncan to E. N. Bell January 19, 1922.

enly voice soaring high above the human voices! This audible manifestation of the invisible One did not produce an unnatural absorption in the unusual, but it would have been strange indeed if every person present on these two occasions did not experience an awed and joyous recognition of the nearness of God. [7]

BETHEL

Bethel Bible Institute was the result of the outpouring of the Spirit upon the month-end spiritual life rallies and the ten-day conferences at Easter and Thanksgiving in the Bethel Pentecostal Tabernacle in Newark, New Jersey. In 1916 Allan Swift, the Bethel pastor; Christian Lucas, Ossining, New York, pastor, and Minnie Draper, a former CMA executive, organized a school for the training of Pentecostal young people as ministers and missionaries. W. W. Simpson, famed missionary to China, was chosen as the first principal. When Simpson returned to the field in 1918, Frank M. Boyd succeeded him, remaining at Bethel until 1923, when he left to head the newly formed Central Bible Institute in Springfield. William I. Evans assumed the post after Boyd's departure, and directed Bethel until 1929, when the school amalgamated with Central Bible Institute.

Frank Mathews Boyd was a product of the Pentecostal effusion at Nyack. If ever a man was "called" into a teaching ministry, Boyd was that man. Three years under A. B. Simpson, additional training years later at Los Angeles Pacific College, and a lifelong study of the Scriptures equipped this man for a Bible school teaching career which has now extended over a period of forty-four years. A military bearing and a firm insistence upon the observance of regulations have sometimes given an impression of a stern disciplinarian, but firmness has been combined with a deep sympathy and understanding of the problems of students. Numerous students recall how the scholarly and dignified Boyd, despite his Presbyterian background, would

---

[7] This firsthand report was given to the author by a number of the students who witnessed this supernatural event, including Ralph M. Riggs, certainly not a man given to hallucinations.

become so ecstatic on occasion that he danced in the Spirit and led "Jericho marches"! Frank Boyd was the originator and director for many years of the Assemblies of God Bible Correspondence Courses. He is also the author of many splendid volumes which have served as textbooks in a number of the schools and blessed the whole Movement. Students by the thousand rise up to call this man blessed— this man who at 77 was still a vigorous tennis player!

Bethel Bible Institute, in its fourteen years of separate existence, trained some of the best-known pastors, evangelists, missionaries, and officials in the Assemblies of God. Two young men with dissimilar backgrounds but with exceptional futures were welcomed to this school. The first was an orphan whose boyhood days were replete with hardships and who, like Horatio Alger, had to make his own way. His insatiable desire for knowledge and his exceptional ability to impart truth soon brought him into prominence as a Pentecostal Apollos, a favorite of camp meetings from coast to coast, a preacher whose eloquence was surpassed only by the prophetic utterances which the Holy Spirit poured through his lips—Harry J. Steil.

The second young man was surrounded by a happy Christian home life, the son of a leading Pentecostal minister, and the beloved brother of two lovely sisters. He was a crack athlete and especially good at swimming. The championship swimming meet of his western Canadian province was scheduled during the time of a revival campaign in his father's church. His father was too busy to attend the contest, and perhaps would not have been too keen about attending if he had been free. The evangelist, however, took his off-night to watch the competition and to cheer his young friend on to victory. Standing outside the gymnasium in sub-zero weather, trophy in hand, the new swimming champion looked at his "Barnabas," and asked, "Say, what would I have to do to become a preacher?" It was the first interest the boy had ever shown in the ministry, and this despite the fact that his victory that evening had brought the offer of athletic scholarships and a career in sports. The evangelist was David McDowell, and the teen-age youth was Watson Argue. Encouraged to attend Bethel, Watson quickly forged to the front of the ministerial ranks to become one of the most successful pastors and evangelists in the entire Pentecostal Movement —and much of the credit is due to the friendly interest of an older Christian at a crucial time in his young life. [8]

Parental opposition often had to be overcome by the students in order to attend Bible school. Florence Barton had gone to the Pentecostal tent meeting in her hometown of Evansville, Indiana, to "see the show," but conviction gripped her heart and she surrendered to the Lord. When she disclosed her desire to enroll at Bethel, her father refused to let her go all the way back East to "one of those crazy Pentecostal schools." No arguments, pleas, or tears could move him, so Florence sadly committed her future to the Lord, and He began to work. The only earthquake in Evansville's history temporarily softened the father's heart, but as the time for registration grew near, his pride reasserted itself. This time he was smitten with a grievous affliction which no physician could diagnose, and realizing that this was indeed the hand of God upon him for his hard heart, Mr. Barton confessed his stubbornness, asked for forgiveness, and was immediately healed— and Florence came to Bethel! [9]

GLAD TIDINGS

Glad Tidings Bible Institute began as a new converts' class in the downtown San Francisco mission conducted by Robert J. and Mary Craig. The class outgrew one room after another, until it had to be moved to the main room of a former saloon on O'Farrell Street. A three-story edifice was secured with enough rooms to accommodate the students as well as provide classroom space. Each student assessed himself five cents per day toward the rent, which proved to be almost enough to pay for the entire year.

Sacrifice for Christ was exemplified by the Craigs. The

[8] Told to the author by Zelma Argue, September 15, 1959.
[9] Told to the author by Florence Barton Benjamin, April 5, 1958.

same love which caused them to give up their own bed in the early days to some "down and outer" now caused them to refuse the offer of a lovely home in one of the most exclusive sections of the city, in order to be near the work they loved. When Mary Craig received an $80,000 inheritance, she immediately invested it in a downtown property upon which was erected a modern, fireproof, six story concrete building with an auditorium seating about 1,500, not including a 200-voice choir and a 40-piece orchestra. In 1925 Glad Tidings ventured into the new field of gospel broadcasting by placing two 100-foot towers on top of its building, and began to send forth the full gospel over its own station KGTT.

The Craigs gave thirty years to this great work in San Francisco. Both were excellent teachers and both had a great vision for the lost. This combination made Glad Tidings through the years a center of Bible scholarship and practical evangelism. Street meetings, jail services, and meetings every night of the year in the huge auditorium produced thousands of graduates whose hearts were aflame and who knew how to win souls to Christ—men like Emil Balliet, Ted Ness, Lloyd Christiansen, and Curtis Ringness.

The ministry of the Craigs was augmented in 1919 by the coming of D. W. Kerr to Glad Tidings. Willard Peirce, Kerr's son-in-law, and a noted pastor, teacher, and exponent of personal evangelism in his own right, also joined the faculty at this time. Other men who have left their mark on Glad Tidings include J. N. Gortner, J. Wesley Cooksey, T. J. Jones, and Leland Keys.

SOUTHERN CALIFORNIA

While at San Francisco, Kerr was asked by Harold Needham, of Los Angeles, to consider opening a school in Southern California. The Needhams, who were planning a world itinerary, offered to put their large house at Kerr's disposal for the use as the first home of Southern California Bible Institute. Christine Kerr Peirce describes those early days:

Father was approaching the years when he could not bear the entire responsibility, and asked us to pray about joining him in this new venture of faith. So the four of us went to Los Angeles and opened the first summer term of the Southern California Bible School in the Needham residence at 5036 Echo Street, Highland Park. The house was there, but no furniture or furnishings. There was no financial backing, although Bethel Temple and its pastor, Rev. G. N. Eldridge, took the burden on their hearts and gave practically all the help that was received. Later father and Mr. Peirce approached Mr. M. E. Layne, of the Layne-Bowler Pump Corp., concerning the needs of the school and he generously responded, as he and other members of his family continued to do through the Layne Foundation.

During the first summer term of the school over thirty were registered. In those days not much was known about proper titles, but actually Mr. Peirce might have been called Dean of Education, as well as business manager and teacher. The salaries for all teachers and administrators were $50.00 per month—if and when it came in! Father Kerr and Mr. Peirce continued in the operation of the school for two school years. During this time Harold Needham returned from the Orient, after the death of his beloved wife, Huldah, in India. The enrollment grew to about seventy during these two years. [10]

Again, the Kerrs and Peirces helped to lay a good foundation, and Harold Needham proved to be a man who could build wisely upon that foundation. His ministry was supplemented through the years by John Wright Follette, Frank M. Boyd, Irvine J. Harrison, O. Cope Budge, and other excellent teachers and administrators. The missionary vision of this school has been outstanding: the percentage of graduates entering missionary service is said to exceed that of any other Assemblies of God school—an enviable record indeed!

CENTRAL BIBLE INSTITUTE [11]

The desire had been often expressed for a General Council school, preferably located in the central part of the nation. An abortive attempt in this direction was made by the establishing of the Midwest Bible School at Auburn, Nebraska, in 1920, with S. A. Jamieson as the principal. However, from its very beginning there did not seem to be the providential confirmation that attends the true leading of the Lord. Capable teachers were difficult to find,

---

[10] Christine Kerr Peirce, *op. cit.*
[11] Name changed to Central Bible College, 1964.

and opening day had to be delayed once by a coal strike and again by an epidemic which caused the mayor to quarantine the city. Too, the Assemblies of God had little representation on the Board of Directors: only two votes out of eleven. Consequently, the 1921 General Council decided to open a school of its own elsewhere.

Meanwhile in Springfield, Missouri, the North End Commerical Club was instrumental in securing fifteen acres of land as a gift to the Assemblies of God for a Bible school. This action seemed to signal divine approval upon the decision of the brethren to locate the school in the headquarters city. God also worked on both ends of the line concerning the faculty. In Los Angeles, "Father Kerr would often speak of the longing of his heart to see a Bible institute at headquarters. Talking to us one day, he said, 'I feel like Simeon of old. If I could just see a Bible school at Springfield, I could say, Now lettest Thou Thy servant depart in peace.' " [12] This dream was soon to be realized, for the invitation was extended by E. N. Bell to Kerr and Peirce to establish this General Council school, to be known as Central Bible Institute.

Central Assembly at Campbell and Calhoun Streets became the temporary home of the school. Kerr went to work alongside other staff members, using shovel, trowel, and paint brush to prepare the basement for the thirty-five or forty students who would need classroom, kitchen, and dining room space. A year later, Frank M. Boyd was called from the East to lead the school, as Kerr's health began to fail. The work that God had given Daniel Warren Kerr to do was almost finished. But what a work! Personally saving the Assemblies of God twice from assuming an unscriptural position on doctrine, Kerr now had participated in the founding of three Bible institutes in which truth could be committed unto faithful men who were able to teach others also.

It would be difficult indeed to assess the value of Central Bible Institute to the Assemblies of God. Its favored position as the only General Council Bible school and its

---

[12] *Ibid.*

location at headquarters have served to attract students from all over the world; its faculty members have had a ministry that has extended far beyond the borders of the school itself; its graduates are numbered among those who "sit in the gates" in every area of ministry.

One CBI student who later became an instructor at his alma mater was destined to a great ministry: a young Jewish lad, Myer Pearlman. Born in Edinburgh, Scotland, on December 19, 1898, Myer was "an Hebrew of the Hebrews," educated in Jewish schools and filled with antipathy toward Christianity. After his immigration to America, however, he was drawn, step by step, to Jesus of Nazareth. Standing one evening outside Glad Tidings Mission in San Francisco, Pearlman listened to the congregation sing, "Honey in the Rock," composed by his father-in-law-to-be, F. A. Graves. He felt himself irresistibly drawn inside this mission where the people were singing so joyfully. How he accepted Christ, Pearlman himself described:

I was not worked up emotionally, nor was I expecting anything to happen, nor was I praying. As I stood there, I felt some strange influence come over me, indescribable but delightful. I saw no one and heard no audible voice. But this was the turning point in my life! My journey to the unknown sanctuary was ended. I had found the reality of Christ. As I knelt to pray one day not too long afterward, to my amazement I heard myself speaking words unfamiliar to me (Pearlman was proficient in Hebrew, Greek, Spanish, French and Italian). It lifted me into a higher realm and gave me a sense of the nearness of God.[13]

Now a Spirit-filled Christian, Pearlman studied briefly at Glad Tidings, and then followed Kerr to Springfield, where he enrolled in Central Bible Institute for its first year, in 1922. This quiet, studious youth soon won the hearts of faculty and students. A tragic accident during his student days gave him a sense of destiny. Scheduled to ride to an outstation one Sunday morning for a service, Myer was asked at the last moment to change places with another youth. His substitute was killed that day in the very automobile seat which Pearlman would have occupied.

Following his graduation, Myer was asked to join the

---

[13] "My Journey to the Unknown Sanctuary," *Pentecostal Evangel*, July 31, 1943.

faculty. Thus he launched upon a teaching career that was to mean much to the Assemblies of God and a writing career that was to bless millions. As a teacher, Pearlman was so distressed by the possibility that he might bore his classes that he searched far and wide for interesting material. The freshness, simplicity, and balance of his presentation gave his lectures a lasting quality. Unusually considerate of the feelings of his students, Pearlman endeavored to keep them from "losing face." When an answer was wide of the mark, he would kindly proceed to reword the answer in such a way that it included the facts. This approach occasionally produced a rueful smile from a student who knew full well that, while the answer placed in his mouth by Pearlman now contained the right words, it certainly was not what the student was trying to say!

The payless summers between semesters were a source of deep anxiety to the young teacher with his growing family. To bolster the exchequer, he volunteered his services as a writer of the *Adult Student's Quarterly*. Soon he was given the task of preparing the *Teacher's Quarterly*. Alternating between the school in the morning and the Gospel Publishing House in the afternoon, Pearlman was a tireless, conscientious worker. Soon, he was working far into the night with his "hunt and peck" system of typing to turn out a series of books that were a fund of information and inspiration to the young movement. His greatest literary contribution was, undoubtedly, the servicemen's publication during World War II, *Reveille*, which was so highly praised by all chaplains and so popular among the men that 14 million copies were distributed.

Myer Pearlman suffered the same frustration felt by many teachers and writers whose ministry is largely confined to a desk. He once confessed to a former student [14] who at the time had a small, struggling church, that he "envied" him the opportunity to minister directly to the people. Through the summer months Pearlman taught large audiences in camp meetings across the nation, but this was too similar to the classroom to make him completely happy.

---

[14] Harry C. Wiles, personal interview, December 10, 1960.

When he did find a spare moment for personal witnessing, he seized it with alacrity.

One night Mrs. Pearlman heard voices outside their home. Looking out, she saw her husband and a youth, whom he had met at the public library, in deep, earnest discussion. The young man was not a Christian, but his clear, logical mind and his searching questions caused Pearlman to covet him for the Lord. Long after midnight, he was able to lead the youth, a "kid brother" of Mrs. Ralph Riggs and Fred Merian (veteran missionary to India), to the Lord. Jimmy Merian was stricken with a fatal disease, and it was a heartbroken Pearlman who stood to speak a few months later at the funeral. But what a joy it was for this teacher, who so frequently felt that his teaching was mostly theory, to refer to his young friend whom he had personally led to Christ as *"Brother* Merian"!

The man who served as Dean of Central Bible Institute from 1929 to 1952, William I. Evans, was unquestionably the chief cause for the spiritual reputation of the school. Evans was a spiritual giant, a man with an enormous capacity for the things of God and with a tremendous ability to communicate them by his godly life and his classroom and platform ministry. Known through the Movement for his teaching at conferences and camp meetings, for his voice lifted on the Council floor on behalf of spiritual realities, and for his anointed writings and radio messages, Evans was known to his students as a man who knew the leading of the Spirit in the great awakenings at Bethel and CBI. Time and time again he directed the attention of all to Calvary, spoke a word which loosed all in the Spirit, or gave forth a truth in those hallowed hours which proved to be "words to live by." Other schools have had their counterparts of William I. Evans, but none surpassed him. The following eloquent tribute, penned by a CBI alumnus, L. B. Richardson,[15] speaks for thousands of those who sat at the feet of this man of God:

---

[15] Pastor and General Presbyter.

I walked through silent halls at night
The lights were low, all voices still—
Then in the reaches of my soul, a chord was struck
And memory came at will.

I saw the halls and classes throb with life;
I heard the songs and felt prayer's after-glow
Above the rush and move I heard the voice now still—
"This stream must flow."

Then viewing far I saw a thousandfold
This message go
In ministries of those whose lives he touched
The message echoed, "This stream must flow."

Above the rank and file of men he lived,
His realm the Holy Ghost;
He stood and thundered forth alone,
This Dean of Pentecost.

Then suddenly the silence came;
The lights again were low,
And deep within, I felt the message of his life—
"This stream must flow." [16]

---

[16] *The Cup*, (C.B.I. annual), 1952.

CHAPTER 10

SOWERS OF THE WORD

THE TWENTIES witnessed an alarming decline in Sunday school and church attendance in most old-line denominations. It became less difficult for Satan to take away the Word sown in hearts, as Darwinism succeeded in creating an indifference to a literal interpretation of the Scriptures. A postwar reaction against the grim realities of life produced a shallowness which was not conducive to true religion. Thorns of material prosperity and worldly pleasure sprang up and choked the Word. Once "well-watered fields" suffered under a prolonged drought, and locusts devoured the land.

Spiritual farmers were needed: men who could plow deep, sow good seed, hoe out thorns, pray down rain, and thrust in the sickle—and God supplied the need. "From the mountains, to the prairies, to the oceans white with foam," the Lord thrust forth laborers into the fields, and how He blessed their earnest efforts, opening the windows of heaven upon them, rebuking the devourer, and giving His servants an abundant harvest!

THE EAST

The Eastern Seaboard loomed large on the Assemblies of God skyline in the twenties. Some of the strongest churches were located in this area, and they shared the unchallenged position that the East enjoyed before the tremendous shift of population westward. Men with wide influence in the fellowship were active in this sector of the nation.

Glad Tidings Tabernacle, of New York City, made a giant stride forward in 1921 with the purchase of the brick church formerly known as Calvary Baptist Church, on West 33rd Street near the Pennsylvania Station. Within four years, Pastor Robert Brown happily conducted the "funeral" service of the two mortgages totalling $70,000:

Since it hath pleased Almighty God to remove from the earth these two hindrances to the spread of the gospel, I therefore commit their bodies to the flame, ashes to ashes, dust to dust! [1]

Now free from debt, the congregation was able to devote its sacrificial gifts to missions in such measure that, for many years, Glad Tidings led all assemblies in annual giving to the cause so dear to the Master's heart.

Dr. John Roach Straton, pastor of Calvary Baptist Church, also of New York City, evoked a sensation during this period by advocating the Pentecostal experience. The reception of the Spirit's fullness by his son Warren in the church in the summer of 1927 precipitated a crisis in this evangelical congregation! The church chose to remain non-Pentecostal, but Warren himself was precipitated into the ministry of the Assemblies of God, and at present is a most talented instructor in Evangel College. [2]

Calvary Baptist Church, of Washington, D. C., made its contribution to the Assemblies of God. The teacher of the Men's Bible Class, Harry L. Collier, was startled to hear his mother testify in 1907 that she had been baptized in the Holy Spirit in the same manner as the early disciples. He was profoundly impressed by the new power which radiated from her, but something within him rebelled against receiving this experience for himself. To avoid the necessity of making a decision Collier drifted into a worldly condition, but the chastening hand of the Lord quickly brought him to repentance. A thorough search of the Scriptures confirmed his mother's testimony, and soon the reality of his own experience dispelled all doubts. When God called him to preach the full gospel, Collier responded with gladness of heart.

His first sermonic efforts were offered in a tiny mission

---

[1] *Pentecostal Evangel.*
[2] Warren Straton died in 1966 as a result of an auto accident.

on Water Street, where frequently his only listener was his patient and loving wife. Refusing to sink in the "Slough of Despond," Collier steadfastly continued to declare the "apostles' doctrine" by night while he worked for the government by day. Slowly but surely, the congregation grew until it was forced to move twice to larger quarters: first to a larger mission on Pennsylvania Avenue, and second, to a fully equipped former Methodist church at North Capitol and K Streets. For twenty-five years Harry L. Collier pastored the Full Gospel Tabernacle. A man of extraordinary spiritual capacity, Collier was mightily anointed to lead his congregation in worship "like to that above" in its purity and power. He succeeded, furthermore, in making the Tabernacle the best-known center of evangelism in the nation's capital.

The members of the congregation reflected the vision of their pastor in many unique ways. Commander Thomas Hewson was attached to the expedition which Admiral Richard E. Byrd led to the North Pole in 1926. When his hand was so severely crushed in an accident that an amputation seemed imperative, Hewson determined to trust God for its healing, and within twenty-four hours the hand was perfectly whole. A Norwegian ship pilot, Esak Isaksen, made an "impossible" leap from an ice floe to safety, and tearfully embraced Hewson who was fervently and audibly praying for his safety, acknowledging that it was God who had saved him from an icy grave. A copy of the Tabernacle's monthly magazine, "Full Gospel Messenger," was carried by Hewson, as with the other members of the party he came to the Pole itself; thus making a Pentecostal publication the first piece of Gospel literature to reach that uttermost part of the earth.

Linwood ("Jack") Safford, a former football player at Bates College, made a lasting impression upon the boys who were in his Sunday school class at the Full Gospel Tabernacle. Jack won their hearts by taking time to play football and baseball with the lads on Saturdays. Morning and evening, he mentioned each one in prayer. If the boys were not sitting with their parents on Sunday morning, Jack herded them into a bench, and "compelled" them to go forward with him, where at the altar with his arm around first one and then another, he poured out his heart for his boys. Is it any wonder that at least twelve of those lads in whom Jack took such an interest are today Pentecostal preachers? Or is it strange that this man who gave up his Saturdays, which as a salesman with a large family to support he could ill-afford to do, now owns a prosperous business?

On December 11, 1926, a young lad of 13 years lay gasping for breath in a Washington suburb. This victim of pulmonary tuberculosis knew that his life was ebbing away. For weeks, his daily routine had consisted of chills, fever, sweats, and hemorrhages. A group of saints from the Full Gospel Tabernacle gathered on this wintry day for one last desperate. prayer. It was now or never. Thank God, it was *now!* God heard and answered prayer. The glory of the Lord filled the room and "the power of the Lord was present to heal." In a short time, the teen-ager was playing football with his pals, healthy and happy again. God's hand continued to rest upon this lad, who today is a successful pastor and teacher, foreign missions counselor, and writer of the notes on the Sunday school lesson in *The Pentecostal Evangel*—J. Bashford Bishop.

The Highway Mission Tabernacle, of Philadelphia, Pennsylvania, was founded in 1894 by Frederick Reel, an auditor with the Reading Railroad. Reel brought his congregation into the Pentecostal Movement in 1906, and in due time into the Assemblies of God. In addition to sending forth. scores of ministers and missionaries, this church has the distinction of being the only assembly to contribute two of its pastors to the fellowship as General Superintendents: Ernest S. Williams and Wesley P. Steelberg.

It was during Williams' ministry (1920-1930) that Highway experienced its greatest growth. The huge gothic structure at 19th and Green streets was purchased in 1924, and was destined to be used for the entertainment of the 1933 General Council. Williams' previous pastorates had been in rather small churches. He had served the church in Bradford, Pennsylvania, where he was compelled to walk seven miles to and from each service. From Bradford, he went to Newark, New Jersey, to serve Bethel, the church that was related to the Bethel Bible School in that city. It was during the period of his sojourn in Newark that his ministry attracted the attention of the members of the Board of Highway Mission Tabernacle in Philadelphia and resulted in a call to serve that church. The ten-year sojourn in the "City of Brotherly Love" proved to be a training ground for the ministry of General Superintendent, to which he was called in the 1929 General Council in Wichita, Kansas.

Highway Tabernacle exemplified a feature of Pentecostal worship which was prevalent in these days: the participation of the entire congregation in the service. It was no "one-man show," nor was it necessary to introduce liturgical rites, in order to insure congregational participation. The members of this Spirit-filled body of believers had something to minister to one another through the exercise of the gifts of the Spirit, inspiring exhortations, psalms, and hymns. But woe betide the person who was "in the flesh" and not "in the Spirit," for this was a perceptive assembly which knew God and had no time for the merely human in worship. The believer who presumed to take unto himself the honor of ministering to the church, who spoke or sang from his own spirit, was immediately told to sit down, or else was sung down!

Ralph Jeffrey, for thirty-nine years pastor of the Bethel Assembly in Hagerstown, Maryland, received his early training in the Spirit-charged atmosphere of Highway Tabernacle. During his ministry in Hagerstown, fourteen new assemblies were organized in the surrounding area, and more than forty ministers and missionaries were sent out by this church, including such outstanding workers as Evangelist Hattie Hammond, Pastor Harry C. Wiles, of Richmond, Va., and J. F. Slye, first Superintendent of the North Carolina District. Other outstanding ministers in the Maryland area were J. E. Kistler and Edward F. M. Staudt, the latter of Baltimore, Maryland.

Jeffrey was a man of constant prayer. Each Saturday,

without fail, he waited upon God from 9 A. M. until 3 P. M.
Visitors in the home tell of going to sleep late at night
with the low rumble of his praying in their ears, only to be
awakened early in the morning by the same sound. No
wonder that upon his public ministry "there came a sound
from heaven"! Although an avid reader of religious books,
Jeffrey was preeminently "a man of one book." He loved
the Word of God, and the supreme thrill of his life was
to declare its unsearchable riches. To fledgling preachers
his counsel was "enjoy your preaching, for it is certain
that, if you don't enjoy it, nobody else will!" Simplicity
was the keynote of his life. This was reflected in his
utter lack of interest in material possessions and personal
ambition which so greatly concern lesser men.

The ministry of this man was much appreciated throughout the East because of its prophetic nature. Like many
of his contemporary Pentecostal brethren, Jeffrey feared
that, through the subtlety of Satan, his mind "should be
corrupted from the simplicity that is in Christ." While not
remiss in preparing his messages, he sought with great
earnestness to preach "present truth," the truth that God
had designed for that particular hour. To do so, Jeffrey
found that he could not be too concerned with the niceties
of homiletics, that he must deliberately jolt his active and
well-informed mind out of its usual patterns of thought, and
in humble and prayerful dependence seek for the higher
thought of God. This method was not always easy on
"the flesh" of the preacher or the people, for he was
occasionally forced to "mark time" until the inspiration
came. Nevertheless, Jeffrey and his like-minded brethren
had learned a secret: the truths that flashed upon their
Scripture-oriented and prayer-saturated minds sped to their
targets with the accuracy and power of lightning bolts.
Consequently, to speak "as they were moved by the Holy
Ghost" became the desire of their hearts, for not only
was it the most effective way to preach, but it was also
a thrilling adventure to learn new truth as it poured forth
from their own lips!

Four young men who were to exercise an above-average
influence upon the Assemblies of God were converted

within a few months of each other in McKeesport, Pennsylvania, in 1914. Frank Lindquist and James Menzie came to the Lord in a Scandinavian church in McKeesport, and shortly afterward began to attend the services directed by the Casley brothers, Frank and Will, under whose ministry "Big Ben" Mahan and "Little Ben" Hardin were saved. The sovereignty of God was definitely at work in bringing together these four youths each of whom was to have an outstanding ministry.

The sole member of this quartet to minister exclusively in the East was Ben Mahan. The First Pentecostal Church, of Jeannette, which he pioneered, was a key work in western Pennsylvania during the formative period of the Assemblies of God. Like so many assemblies, it had its beginning in a street meeting. Mahan often recalled those open-air services with the hecklers and drunks who made trouble, and yet, with such a glory upon the people that it was easy for him to minister effectively. A man with rugged convictions, a preacher of solid Bible messages, Mahan witnessed a flourishing growth in his nineteen years of ministry in Jeannette, and later in seventeen years at the Full Gospel Tabernacle in Washington, D. C. His practical philosophy was revealed in the reply he gave to a friend who once exclaimed about the size of his reward for his abundant labors in the ministry:

I have sought to do what God wanted me to do, and undoubtedly, there will be a reward for me, as the Lord has promised; but I am sure that there will be just as big a reward for the man who, in the will of God, spent his life digging ditches! [3]

A chief characteristic of the saints of God in these days was their intense desire to be baptized in the Holy Ghost, and the Lord baptized some of them in the most unlikely places. William L. Couzens, a blacksmith and a member of the Scranton, Pennsylvania, assembly, was shoeing a mule deep in a coal mine in the summer of 1921, when God gave him the desire of his heart. That poor mule had heard all kinds of language but never anything like this torrent of eloquence in another tongue. This was

---

[3] Quoted by Mrs. Ben Mahan to the author, January 12, 1960.

probably the only time when a blacksmith got so happy
in a coal mine that he left a bewildered mule and ran
along the coal-car tracks to the surface, speaking in tongues
and magnifying God! William Couzens kept right on rejoicing through the years, and became an evangelist who
was billed as *The Happy Welshman.*

Louis Schap, a fellow member of the Scranton assembly,
was a fireman at this time on the Erie Railroad. Schap
was busily firing the boiler, as the engine labored up a
long mountain grade, when the Spirit of God came upon
him. The fireman was set on fire! So consumed was Schap
by his own great need of God and by the glory that flamed
in his soul, that he forgot all about his firing duty. The
train made the grade, even though it was without the fireman whose best efforts were normally required all the way
to the top. This time it must have been God who lifted
both train and trainman to higher ground! [4]

These days were not without their humorous incidents.
C. Stanley Cooke, a noted evangelist in later years, suffered
a rather embarrassing "Eutychus experience," while serving
as a song leader in a Swanton, Maryland, revival in 1922.
The meetings were being conducted in a "glory barn" (and
this was no mere euphemism). The top of a haystack was
the only place young Cooke could find to be seated after
his song-leading chore was finished. Edgar Barrick, missionary to India, preached the message and extended the
invitation:

"Who will be the first to come?"

High on his lofty perch above the "platform," Cooke
blinked sleepily. He shifted his position in the hay. To
his consternation, he felt himself slipping. He could not
stop his downward flight by digging his heels into the hay,
and he would have had to drop his guitar if he had tried
to grab the hay with his hands. Faster and faster slid the
song leader toward the unsuspecting audience below.

"Who will be the first to come?"

With a crash, Cooke hit the altar rail. No longer was

---

[4] Both incidents related by Louis Schap, July 10, 1960.

"every head bowed and every eye closed." After all, it is not too often that one who sang like an angel should descend from above in such a startling manner to answer the altar call! Cooke was not only the first but also the last to respond to the invitation that fateful evening.[5]

Even missionaries learned to smile through their tears. In 1919 Ralph M. Riggs set forth for South Africa, where he was to spend six years ministering to the Venda Tribe, with the promise of fifty dollars support each month—a princely sum for a single youth in those days. Unfortunately, the lady who had made the promise, as a memorial to her son, discovered that she could not afford to send the money, since it cost 50 cents to send the $50 money order! Her letter of explanation brought forth a shocked exclamation from Riggs: "Why, I would have been happy to take $49.50!" Riggs still chuckles to this day over the grim humor of the situation, although months of privation followed as a result of this broken vow. Thank God for the ability to see "the funny side of things," which has enabled all pioneers at home and abroad to laugh in the face of their most discouraging trials of faith.

Up and down the Atlantic Coast pastors were struggling to establish an Assemblies of God beachhead. It was difficult to make much headway in the tradition-bound East, and most of the Assemblies were quite small. Nevertheless, all agreed completely with the words of the inimitable A. G. Ward: "I would rather be the pastor of the smallest Pentecostal incubator than to be Dr. All-Wise, in charge of the largest religious refrigerator!"[6] And God blessed the "incubators," and the numbers of babes in Christ who were nourished there increased as "the Lord added to the church daily."

The Gospel which was preached by these men had little in common with that which a youthful Universalist minister sought to introduce to a large congregation in a New England village about this time.[7] At the close of his sermon,

[5] Personal interview, July 10, 1959.
[6] *Pentecostal Evangel*, May 8, 1926
[7] *Ibid.*

in which he had endeavored to convince his hearers that there is no punishment after death, the preacher informed the people that, if they wished, he could return in four weeks. A merchant rose to his feet and replied, "Sir, if your doctrine is true, we won't need you; and if it is false, we don't want you!"

But these New Englanders did want men like H. T. Carpenter, T. Arthur Lewis, C. C. Garrett, H. H. Shelley, and William Mitchell who "did not shun to declare unto them the whole counsel of God." The Newfoundlanders who settled in the Boston area embraced the Pentecostal message as an extension of the Methodist revival. Who can ever forget their Spirit-filled singing of the traditional Wesleyan hymns? The "Newfies" were not much for choruses, but oh, how they could make the rafters ring with verse after verse of those grand old Methodist songs! One can imagine Charles and John Wesley saying, "This is the way these hymns were meant to be sung!"

E. N. Bell in 1921 attended the first Assemblies of God convention in the region which today comprises the Appalachian District. Reporting on the progress of the full gospel in this beautiful mountain area, Bell wrote, "Pentecost is sweeping the country!"[8] God had been mightily blessing the efforts of such faithful men as L. A. Sappington, J. H. Stroud, H. H. Maynard, George Sprouse, J. E. Brooks, S. W. Sublette, Fred Novak, and C. W. Smith. Working in a region of chronic depression, these heroic men had succeeded in "making many rich."

SOUTHEAST

One of the most unique ministers in the Assemblies of God was mightily used of God to spread Pentecost throughout the Southeastern states: Isaac J. Bolton. A former railroad engineer, Bolton was noted for his reasonable facsimile of a train whistle which he emitted when he got to "feeling religious." He was also famed for his oft-quoted declaration, "If you can't feel *that,* you must be dead!" To say nothing of his rendition of the Beethoven-

---

[8] *Pentecostal Evangel,* July 9, 1921.

like chorus, "I'm under the spout, where the glory comes out!" Utterly uninhibited, gregarious, aggressive, this lantern-jawed Irishman knew just when to bring his short sermons to an abrupt end and to draw in the net. Thousands were converted and filled with the Spirit in his evangelistic ministry, and he was the founder of assemblies in Miama, Tampa, Lakeland, Goulds, and other Florida cities. Ralph Byrd, Mayme Williams, and Emma Taylor were converted in the Tampa Oak Park assembly which he helped to establish and pastored for years. In the midst of all these activities, Bolton still found time to serve in every office of the South Florida District.

Pleasant Grove Camp, at Durant, Florida, was being thrilled by the dynamic preaching of national Pentecostal leaders, and also by local men like A. G. Voight, Sam C. Perry, J. L. Webb, C. W. Hause, and W. E. Emanuel (in the opinion of qualified judges, "Billy" Emanuel is one of the most original and profound preachers ever produced in the Assemblies of God). But the people came, primarily, to meet God. One sixty-four-year-old man rode a bicycle 100 miles through the rain in 1923 to receive the infilling of the Spirit. Gloriously filled, he did not at all mind the long journey home. "The toils of the road" seemed nothing, for he felt as though he were "walking on clouds instead of pushing or pedalling a bike!" [9]

James O. Savell was an outstanding example of the pioneer preacher in the Southland. Evangelist, circuit-riding pastor and district superintendent, Savell left his mark upon Mississippi, Alabama, Louisiana, and Texas. As a youth, he showed promise and was invited both by the Baptists and the Methodists to enter the ministry. His lack of theological training caused him to decline the invitations, but when he was endued with power from on high, this feeling of inadequacy disappeared, and he launched out boldly in 1914 as one of the first Assemblies of God preachers.

His first meeting turned into a genuine revival. The folks in the area of Mississippi where he had spent his

---

[9] *Pentecostal Evangel*, July 15, 1923.

boyhood days turned out in droves to see if "Jimmy" Savell had really learned how to preach. They found out that he knew how to preach the best way—"with the Holy Ghost sent down from Heaven." The power of God fell on the farmers in the field. An unsaved youth who fell asleep during the prolonged altar service woke up shouting the praises of God! A wife whose husband threatened to leave her if she was baptized stood on the bank of the river, weeping as the baptismal service drew to a close. Unable to restrain herself, she cried out: "I don't care what happens, I've got to follow Jesus!" An elderly woman watched her run to the water, and decided that if her neighbor could be baptized in her "Sunday best," so could she. A young man calling on God to save him, rushed into the water. Pandemonium hit the sinners on the bank, as one after another of their number cried out for mercy and plunged into the waters of baptism. "What a shouting on that shore!" Such an extraordinary move of God made it impossible for a public dance to be held in the community for five years.[10]

Like Savell, many other preachers in the Deep South in the twenties were to distinguish themselves in later years as District and General Council officers. D. P. Holloway, known principally for his successful pastorates in Mobile, Alabama, and Cleveland, Ohio, was also a fiery evangelist and convention speaker whose eloquent sermons were punctuated by the joyful shouts of the congregation, and often interrupted by souls rushing to the altar to be saved or filled with the Spirit. Cast in the same mold were E. L. Tanner, J. E. Spence, W. F. Hardwick, J. D. Courtney, S. W. Noles, and a host of other "mighty men."

MIDWEST

The chairmanship of the Central District, which consisted (in the twenties) of Ohio, Indiana, and Michigan, had rotated among four pastors, C. A. McKinney, J. R. Kline, T. K. Leonard, and J. Narver Gortner. This vast area needed a full-time man, but it was almost universally

---

[10] James O. Savell, personal interview, September 2, 1959.

felt that it would be impossible to support him. A number of the ministers disagreed, and courageously offered to share their meager income with Flem Van Meter, who after being elected, was willing to trust God with them for his support. Van Meter, a former member of the board of an Indiana bank, and a hardware merchant, now learned how "the other half" lived, often sleeping in the Model T while on his itineraries. At times he was forced to wire his partners for funds, when the "flivver" broke down or when he was otherwise stranded. The fellow-feeling that was engendered during this five-year period (1925-1930) helped to "break the ice" for full-time superintendents all over the country, which in turn, gave a great boost forward to the Assemblies of God.

John Waggoner pastored the Christian and Missionary Alliance church in Warren, Ohio, until his reception of the fullness of the Spirit at Nyack. Forced to leave his building, Waggoner was heartened to have two families of his members follow their shepherd. The assembly in Warren became noted for its mighty visitation of the Spirit and for its young men who went forth into the Lord's work: Gayle F. Lewis, H. C. Osgood, Charles Shuss, and the two Waggoner sons, Harry and George, who later ministered so compassionately and effectively to the lepers of India.

O. E. Nash, a railway dispatcher, of Zion, Illinois, typified the strong convictions of Pentecostal preachers everywhere. Nash found the mission door locked in Cincinnati, but did that deter him? "God sent me here, and He will open the door." [11] It soon became evident that God had sent Nash to Cincinnati. Discarded braces and crutches hung on the wall, as a result of the Lord stretching forth His hand to heal. A deep sense of the presence of God pervaded this assembly, making its worship services as unusual and powerful as any in the entire Pentecostal Movement. The evangelistic vision of this congregation extended into neighboring Kentucky. Nash and his people lifted their eyes unto the hills and felt a great burden for these souls who, for the most part, were without the genuine

---

[11]Gayle F. Lewis, personal interview, December 10, 1959.

gospel. Turning his home into a "motel," Nash entertained
the workers going to and fro, and was enabled of the
Lord to direct the evangelizing of Eastern Kentucky.[12]

Each of the midwestern states had its leaders whose
exploits time would fail us to mention: *Ohio*: C. A. Mc-
Kinney, of Akron; A. B. Cox, of Dayton; George Bowie, of
Cleveland; Gayle Lewis, of Canton. *Indiana*: John Price,
of Indianapolis; James Menzie, of Gary; Thomas Paino,
of Indianapolis. *Illinois*: Richard and Adele Carmichael,
of Quincy; A. W. Kortkamp, of Alton; Harry Stemme,
Arthur Bell, Andrew Fraser, of Chicago; Adolf Peterson,
Carl M. O'Guin, and Clyde Bailey. *Michigan*: J. R. Kline,
of Detroit; John Kolenda, of Flint; Alvin Branch, of
Battle Creek. *Missouri*: Henry Hoar, of St. Louis; Fred
Lohman, of St. Louis; S. K. Biffle, of Joplin; K. H. Lawson,
of Flat River; John T. Wilson of Springfield; Aaron A.
Wilson, of Puxico and Kansas City;[13] and William H.
Boyles, of Thayer and Carthage. *Kansas*: Fred Vogler,
superintendent of the Kansas District during the twenties,
had a plan for using Bible school graduates for the
opening of new churches, which was very successful. Other
outstanding ministers were W. G. Greisen, William R.
Cooper, A. R. Farley, Joseph Rosselli, Chas. Sheall, S.
H. Patterson, and John H. James. *West Central* (Iowa
and North Missouri) : John Goben, Charles E. Long, Roy
E. Scott, Eugene N. Hastie, W. E. Longdin, and Geo.
A. Comstock.

The message of divine healing was a vital factor in the
rapid expansion of the Assemblies of God. Every pastor
could have submitted a report similar to that which Pastor
Earl W. Clark, of the Fourfold Gospel Tabernacle, Indianapolis, Indiana, sent to the *Pentecostal Evangel*
(January 30, 1926) :

God led Sister Norton to our church. She had a cancer of four

---

[12] The three Vibbert brothers, Hansel, Harry, and Ted, pastors of three of
the finest assemblies in Indiana, were among the nuggets of gold discovered in
"them thar hills."
[13] Wilson, an executive presbyter for thirty years, has been a tower of
strength in the Assemblies of God, blessing conventions from coast to coast with
his dynamic messages, and at the same time, building a huge congregation in
Kansas City.

years' growth on her nose. It raised up like a sponge, was dark purple in color, and all a mass of scabs; the inside of her nose was eaten out, and there was a hole through the upper lip, making it almost impossible for her to eat. She was looking into the grave and had laid out her deed to the cemetery lot, so that, if she was taken suddenly, her children would find it.

They took her out of bed to bring her to the meetings, and God gave her a greater desire to serve Him than her desire to be healed. She yielded herself anew to God, and every night as she entered the tabernacle, she would kneel in the nearest seat and pour her heart out to Him. The night she was anointed and prayed for God instantly touched her, and the pain vanished, but she was still tested because of the terrible appearance which remained on the outside. The healing began at the roots and worked out. Her nose was healed and built up on the inside. Then one day a few weeks later she came in with a new nose! O glory to God! ... Her healing has meant the salvation and reconsecration of her three daughters and their husbands and others. Does it pay to preach the whole gospel? Yes, every time!

Farther west, in Mt. Pleasant, Kansas, the Buffum Evangelistic Party experienced the joy shared by all the revivalistic Pentecostal preachers of that day:

Whole families were swept into the kingdom of God. So many husbands and wives knelt together to seek God. Among the leading families was a man, his wife and three boys. The wife found God, but the husband refused to yield. One day he came in from the field and said to his wife, "Come on, let's go see the preachers." She looked up and saw tears rolling down his cheeks, and, of course, dropped her washing and went with him. When they got to the house, he cried, "O, I give up! I give up!" God saved him right there. His tobacco was given up, his swearing left him, and all his sins were gone! [14]

NORTH CENTRAL

The North Central District—Minnesota, Wisconsin, North Dakota, South Dakota, and Montana—was formed largely through the efforts of Frank Lindquist, James Menzie, and Ben Hardin. These three young men came to Minnesota in 1921, bringing their own tent poles with them all the way from McKeesport, Pennsylvania. The first assembly was established in Brainerd, and soon branch works were begun in Crosby, Ironton, Pillager, Casino,

---

[14] Lillie Buffum, *Pentecostal Evangel*, July 8, 1922.

and Motley. E. N. Bell, the General Chairman, arrived in Brainerd on November 10, 1922, at the invitation of these enterprising young men, to organize the district. C. M. Hanson was elected the first chairman, but Lindquist was given the post the following year, and served twenty-three fruitful years in the office. He also managed to found the Lake Geneva Camp and North Central Bible Institute (serving as its president for 27 years), has participated as a General Presbyter in General Council activities for 37 years, and has pastored the Full Gospel Tabernacle, in Minneapolis, for 35 years!

James Menzie followed Ben Hardin back to Gary, Indiana, where his two lengthy pastorates were blessed of God. His remarkable message, "Make Room for the Holy Ghost," was judged by many to be one of the most significant articles to appear in years in the *Pentecostal Evangel*. Other "mighty men of valor" who were active in the Minnesota area in those days were Fred Frank, B. W. Brannan, Willard H. Pope, G. W. Nielsen, and a former Advent Christian minister, Wesley R. Hurst, whose sons, D. V. and Wesley, Jr., are making a splendid contribution to the Assemblies of God in literary and missionary fields.

At the start of a revival campaign in Granada, Minnesota, in the late summer of 1927, an attempt was made to obtain used songbooks from a denominational church in the town. The pastor vowed: "I'll burn them first!" A. B. Carpenter, the member of his congregation who had made the request, looked steadily at this angry preacher: "Pastor, I've listened to you for years, and you have never made me sorry I was a sinner, the way this young Pentecostal evangelist has done in just a few nights. Goodbye!" Carpenter bought other songbooks and cast his lot with the young preacher who had made him sorrowful unto repentance—Bert Webb.

This decision may have saved Carpenter's life—or restored it. Webb and a group of the Granada believers received an urgent call a few months later to come to the Carpenter home. To all appearances, Carpenter had suffered a fatal heart attack. There was no pulse, no heartbeat,

The Opera House in Hot Springs, Arkansas, site of the first General Council of the Assemblies of God, April 2-12, 1914.

Visitors and delegates at the first General Council of the Assemblies of God

Executive Presbyters elected at the first General Council. Front row (left to right): T.K. Leonard, E. N. Bell, Cyrus B. Fockler. Back row (left to right): J. W. Welch, J. R. Flower, D. C. O. Opperman, H. A. Goss, and M. M. Pinson.

THE
Christian ✠ Evangel

A LATTER-RAIN PENTECOST WEEKLY

Published with the purpose of propogating, and promoting fellow-ship in, a Full Pentecostal Gospel, according to Apostolic Faith and Practice, particularly in the Central States of America and throughout the entire world, by

THE CHRISTIAN EVANGEL PUBLISHING CO.,
PLAINFIELD,   INDIANA.

J. Roswell Flower, Managing Editor, assisted by the pastors of the Pentecostal Assemblies of Indianapolis and a number of Christian Workers, Evangelists, Pastors and Missionaries.

SUBSCRIPTION PRICE: $1.00 per year, 50 cts. for six months, 25 cts. for three months. All foreign countries, including Canada, add 50 cts. per year extra for postage.

All subscriptions should be sent by Postal or Express Money Orders, made payable to The Christian Evangel, Plainfield, Indiana.

Subscriptions, articles for publication, orders for Bibles and books etc. should be addressed to The Christian Evangel and not to the editors to insure prompt attention. Articles for publication should be written on one side of paper and be brief and to the point as far as it is possible.

All matter for publication must reach our office not later than Friday of each week.

Entered as second class matter September 6, 1913, at the postoffice at Plainfield, Indiana, under the Act of March 3, 1879.

The *Christian Evangel,* founded in 1913 by J. Roswell Flower, was a forerunner of the *Pentecostal Evangel.*

Rev. and Mrs. J. R. Flower

The General Presbytery elected at the 1919 General Council, Stone Church, Chicago. Front row (left to right): J. R. Flower, S. A. Jamieson, E. N. Bell, J. W. Welch, J. T. Boddy, S. H. Frodsham, Ellis Banta; second row (left to right): Frank Gray, J. R. Kline, John Goben, D. H. McDowell, R. A. Brown, Joseph Tunmore, F. A. Hale; third row (left to right): O. P. Brann, E. R. Fitzgerald, E. N. Richey, John Coxe, D. W. Kerr, R. J. Craig, Orville Benham, A. P. Collins, and T. K. Leonard.

An early camp meeting at Potomac Park Camp, Falling Waters, W. V.

Bethel Bible School, Newark, N. J., 1929. In the center of the 2nd row are J. Roswell Flower, W. I. Evans, and R. M. Riggs.

Rochester Bible Training School (Elim), Rochester, N. Y.

P. C. Nelson, founder of Southwestern Bible college

Glad Tidings Bible Institute, San Francisco (school later moved to Santa Cruz and renamed Bethany Bible College).

W. I. Evans
Central Bible Institute

Myer Pearlman
Central Bible Institute

Midwest Bible School, Auburn, Nebraska, 1920

Southern California Bible School, 1920

The Gospel Publishing House, 434 W. Pacific, Springfield, Missouri, as it appeared shortly after it was purchased, 1918.

Assemblies of God Headquarters employees, about 1927

J. Z. Kamerer, first manager of Gospel Publishing House, and secretary.

General Council officers in conference about 1927. From left to right: S. H. Frodsham, Arthur Graves, William Faux, J. Z. Kamerer, J. R. Evans, David McDowell, W. T. Gaston, and Noel Perkin.

Mr. and Mrs. S. H. Frodsham and Charles Robinson, editorial office, 1928.

E. N. Bell
1914; 1919-1923

**Chairmen and Superintendents
1914-1929**

A. P. Collins
1914-1915

J. W. Welch
1915-1919; 1923-1925

W. T. Gaston
1925-1929

E. S. Williams
1929-1949

Raymond T. Richey revival, Houston, Texas, 1922. Inset, Richey Evangelistic Party.

Lillian Trasher

Rachel A. Sizelove

Donald Gee

A. G. Ward

F. F. Bosworth

J. O. Savell

1939 General Council, Springfield, Missouri. Left to right: S. H. Frodsham, F. J. Lindquist, Fred Vogler, W. I. Evans, and Frank Gray.

Ben Hardin (left) and two pastors in tent meeting

Mr. and Mrs. J. Narver Gortner

A typical storefront church. This one is Batavia Gospel Tabernacle, Batavia, Wisconsin. E. F. Erdmann, first pastor.

Joseph P. Wannenmacher

Etta Calhoun

Aimee Semple McPherson

John Wright Follette

Smith Wigglesworth

and no warmth in his body. Nonetheless, his pastor and his fellow believers were loath to let this comparatively young man go. A great spirit of boldness gripped them. Death was rebuked in the name of the Lord Jesus Christ. Suddenly, a Presence came into the room. Carpenter sat upright, blinked his eyes, looked around uncomprehendingly, and gave a long, trembling sigh. "Why," he murmured, "did you bring me back?" He began to describe the beauties of the city which he had momentarily visited. His testimony had a tremendous impact upon the community for years afterward. With tears running down his cheeks, Carpenter would struggle to tell what he had seen: "It looked like. . . . Oh, what's the use. I can't tell it!"

How often in these pioneering days expected help failed to materialize, while last-minute assistance came from the most unexpected sources. A persistent gentleman had begged Bert Webb to come to Appleton, Wisconsin, but when Webb finally accepted the invitation, his would-be-host had moved to Chicago, leaving Webb to pay for the freight of the tent and other miscellaneous items. The meeting which began so dismally for the young evangelist got even worse. No crowds, no conversions, no money. Webb was ready to leave, but, despite the forbidding circumstances, he felt that God was not through with him in Appleton.

A quartet of negro youths from the Piney Woods School, in Piney Woods, Mississippi, came by the tent, and seeing the young evangelist, said, "We would like to sing at your meeting."

Webb protested: "Boys, there aren't enough people to hold church, and no money either."

They looked at each other: "We still feel that God wants us to sing here."

"Well, all right," Webb replied, "but all I can do is to put an ad in the paper and give you half of whatever comes in."

The price of the ad was saved by the editor who printed the story as a news item. And lo! the tent was full, and how the boys sang! The evangelist, unaccustomed as he was in

Appleton to speaking to a crowd, gave a rousing message on repentance. Twenty came to the altar for salvation, as the quartet sang, "Come Home, O Sinner." The revival was on, and another Assembly of God planted. "God moves in mysterious ways, His wonders to perform."[15]

Joseph Wannenmacher, whose anointed ministry and singing violin "made Milwaukee famous" to Assemblies of God people, was a bright and shining light in the Dairy State of Wisconsin.

In Nebraska, G. W. Clopine, H. L. Harvey, Jos. Rediger, Edgar White, A. R. Shaffer, and A. M. Alber were opening the way for the full gospel, while in North and South Dakota, Arthur Berg (a convert of William Durham), C. A. Beebe, Adam Slagel, W. J. George, Albert Howell, P. B. Thompson, Fred Frank, Blanche Brittain, Clara Van Gilder, and Etta E. Reckley were spreading the glad story.

During the fall of 1920 an evangelistic party composed of the Franks, Etta Reckley, and Clara Van Gilder came to Trygg Township, North Dakota, for a revival campaign. Through the blizzards the people drove their horses and sleighs to the schoolhouse. The water in the radiators of the few Model T's which were able to struggle through the drifts was drained into buckets and placed beside the potbellied stove to keep from freezing. Charles Trygg, a prosperous Christian farmer after whom the community was named, received a powerful baptism in the Spirit and decided to "join up with these Pentecostal people." Herman G. Johnson, later to be elected the first District Superintendent of North Dakota, also received the Spirit's fullness in the first outpouring of the Spirit upon this campaign, when literally as in an earlier century, "the place was shaken where they were assembled together." Two children of Charles Trygg are in the ministry today, as a result of this "out of season" revival meeting: Pastor Elmer Trygg, of Shelby, Montana, and Mildred Trygg Smuland, wife of the late Superintendent of the New England

---

[15] Personal interview, Bert Webb, December 15, 1959. Three girls who were saved in this revival became missionaries: Hilda Reffke, Adeline Wickman, and Claudia Dell.

District, Roy Smuland, and former National Secretary of the Women's Missionary Council. [16]

Etta E. Reckley, who helped to found the assemblies in Minot, North Dakota, and Miles City, Montana, and who conducted revival campaigns throughout the entire country, was a woman who "walked with God." The supernatural quality of her meetings surpassed many of those who, in the natural, were better qualified. "Mother" Reckley testified [17] that for a period of twelve years she knew that she did not consciously disobey God in any manner. This period of perfect obedience was momentarily halted by an assertion of her own will in a manner that most Christians would consider too trivial to confess. Nevertheless, after this she continued to be an "example of the believer." *Twelve years!* How many believers can honestly say that for one day, one week, one month or one year they have done "always those things which please the Father"? Yet, Etta Reckley regarded those twelve years as the *normal* way of life for every child of God. It was not easy to keep her German temper in check, when forced to live in "sod houses" which were a far cry from her comfortable home back East; or to stand by patiently while storekeepers deliberately waited first on customers who had come into the store after her and, only when the last one had departed, roughly ask this "Pentecostal person" what she wanted. "But grace and truth came by Jesus Christ." Etta Reckley was indeed a most unforgettable person.

Montana also enjoyed the ministry of such stalwarts as Maurice McGinnis, Luther Powell, D. R. Miller, M. D. Jeffers, A. A. Howell, Joseph Lantz, and W. Paul Jones, who became district superintendent.

SOUTHWEST

Arkansas, the cradle of the Assemblies of God, experienced a rapid growth in the twenties. W. Jethro Walthall, T. J. Gotcher, E. J. Bruton, L. L. Riley, C. A. Lasater, E. R. Fitzgerald, and Wm. D. Burris were prominent

---

[16] Mrs. Mildred Trygg Smuland, personal interview, December 8, 1959.
[17] The author spent many edifying hours in his youth conversing with this "mother in Israel."

leaders in the Razorback State. By 1924, the District Council sessions were so well attended that various cities in Arkansas were bidding for the annual gatherings.

Stephen Vandermerwe, a Boer from South Africa,[18] reported a revival campaign in Dover, Arkansas,

commonly known as a gospel-hardened center. Seventeen were saved and two received the Holy Ghost. Praise God! I held the meeting in an old blacksmith shop, the only available place in town, and although not as fine a place in which to worship as the regular churches, it became the most beautiful church in the world to the ones that made peace with God there.[19]

The work in *Oklahoma* grew so phenomenally that it soon became one of the strongest states in the fellowship. Glenn and Gordon Millard were boy preachers who together with their father, Chas. W. Millard, took the full gospel to Quinlin, Mooreland, Woodward, and surrounding counties. W. F. Garvin, Presbyterian minister, became a Pentecostal minister, establishing a splendid assembly, Faith Tabernacle, in Tulsa.

Dexter Collins was typical of many preachers of this era. A paving contractor who was converted under the ministry of W. T. Gaston in Tulsa, Collins felt the call of God in his life, but hesitated to enter the multifaceted life of a minister. At last, he launched out in the small town of Wellston (population 600). He could not have chosen a rougher or tougher community, a throwback to the Old West of frontier days. Collins was no pulpit orator, but he prayed and persuaded others to pray. Three hundred souls were converted, and approximately twenty ministers and wives of ministers were produced by this church, including Otis Keener, Paul Ralstin, W. Hobson Kennemer, C. O. Haymaker, Bert Webb, Mrs. Glenn Millard, and Mrs. Roy Sprague. "Uncle Jake" Miller came to Wellston, as Peter and John came to Samaria, to "pray for them that they might receive the Holy Ghost." *One hundred twenty,*

---

[18] His native tongue is Afrikaans. However, according to Pastor E. L. Tanner: "A well-educated young man who has no trouble in holding the attention of his audience . . . a real Pentecostal preacher." (*Pentecostal Evangel*, July 17, 1926).

[19] *Pentecostal Evangel*, December 19, 1925.

by actual count, received! "Uncle Jake" probably referred to this campaign as "a real gully-washer!"[20] Other prominent ministers included Byrl Dodd, Oscar Jones, John A. Linn, Floyd L. Hawkins, John W. Hudson, and James S. Hutsell.

What a star-studded cast graced the Texas scene! F. D. Davis, A. C. (5'17") Bates, E. L. Newby, Rewel Newby, Fred and John Eiting, H. H. Wray, E. N. Richey, W. B. McCafferty, G. C. Magrum, T. D. Thompson, J. C. Wilder, O. W. Edwards, E. R. Foster, Harry Bowley, E. C. Crump, and H. M. Cadwalder. Eternity alone will reveal the extent of the ministry of these men of God and a host of others who "by faith, they like a whirlwind's breath, swept on o'er every field."

In Kingsville, Texas, in 1911, a fifteen-year-old lad felt a great burden for the Spanish-American people. As a Methodist, H. C. Ball had worked among "the strangers within our gates," but with the baptism in the Spirit, he was set on fire for their souls. His ability to *hablar espanol* was limited to a simple invitation to come to the little church which he had repaired and scrubbed, a memorized hymn which he sang over and over again, and a badly accented attempt to read from the Spanish Bible. Despite the uproarious laughter that sometimes greeted his linguistic efforts, and despite the hurricane that destroyed the little chapel, Ball would not be denied. God rewarded him with thirteen converts in six months, and on July 4, 1915, after His youthful servant had baptized the converts in water, He baptized nine of them in the Holy Ghost. By the twenties, the work had spread to both sides of the border, with publishing of Spanish literature and Bible schools multiplying the full-gospel witness.

An entire volume could be written about the wondrous compassion and indefatigable labors of this remarkable man. Of course, H. C. Ball did not work alone. Associated with him in this Latin American work in four states (Texas, New Mexico, Arizona, and California) were his devoted wife, Mrs. Sunshine Ball, Alice Luce, Floyd

---

[20] Bert Webb, *op. cit.*

Baker, M. M. Pinson, Einar Peterson and innumerable Spanish brethren—all of whom deserve much credit for the phenomenal success of this work.

New Mexico and *Arizona* were pioneered by B. B. Evans, L. H. Hauff, S. S. Scull, and John Eiting (under Eiting's ministry the parents of Klaude Kendrick, one of the finest Assemblies of God educators and authors, were converted). *Colorado* was blessed by the ministry of W. M. Stevens, F. C. Woodworth, Eric and William Booth-Clibborn, John McConnell, H. B. Garlock, O. L. Mabry, and the Morton Sisters. In *California's* hall of fame: Max Friemark, Wesley R. Steelberg, Carl Hatch, W. C. Anderson, Louis Turnbull, M. T. Draper, Arthur S. Osterberg, Lloyd and Harold Persing, the Weston Brothers, Manuel Sequeira, W. F. A. Gierke, Eric Johnson, and J. D. Wells.

NORTHWEST

Trail blazers in the great Northwest included: *Oregon*: George Bacon, Fred Snyder, O. R. Cross, Lester Carlsen, and Will C. Trotter. *Idaho*: Wesley F. Morton, Thomas Wayne, Oren Channer, H. E. Hansen, and Allan J. Brown. *Washington*: Frank Gray, J. E. Rasmussen, Carl G. Carlson, J. E. Secrist, J. S. Eaton, D. W. Raines, Frank Lindblad, Mrs. Emma Van Dalen Jones, and Mrs. Margaret Finch. The huge campaigns of Dr. Charles S. Price were a major factor in the growth of the Assemblies of God here.

CANADA

For ten years after Hot Springs, Canada was an integral part of the Assemblies of God. H. M. Cadwalder served as an early superintendent of the western provinces, and other American brethren helped to organize the work in the eastern provinces. It was inevitable, however, and desirable that Canada should eventually form its own organization. Accordingly, the two good neighbors extended the right hand of fellowship across the border and upon the world religious scene marched one of the most vigorous full-gospel movements, the Pentecostal Assemblies of Canada.

The Assemblies of God has continued to serve the great

Dominion to the North by supplying much of its Sunday school literature and by sending forth a long list of ministers who have accepted with delight the invitation to labor together with their Canadian brethren. Pastors from the United States like W. C. Peirce and William Kautz have been instrumental in buying or building some of the largest edifices in the Canadian organization. Still, it is extremely doubtful whether the Assemblies of God will ever be able to repay the Land of the Maple Leaf for its loan to us of A. G. Ward, A. H. Argue, R. E. McAlister, Jack Saunders, and Tom Johnstone; and for its gift to us of J. Roswell Flower, Noel Perkin, C. M. Ward, C. W. H. and Douglas Scott, Watson and Zelma Argue, Robert C. Cunningham, Lester Smith, Harvey McAlister, Louis Turnbull, Aimee McPherson, Lorne Fox, Willard and Paul Cantelon, Wallace Bragg, G. Raymond Carlson, R. E. Sternall, C. S. Tubby, Gwen Jones, and Tom Miller.

NATIONAL EVANGELISTS

Two women evangelists made a major impact upon the Pentecostal Movement: the first, *Mary Woodworth Etter*, whose ministry was at its height during the first fifteen years of the Pentecostal outpouring. Countless assemblies ,sprang up in communities across the nation after a visit from Mrs. Etter, who "looked just like your grandmother," but who exercised tremendous spiritual authority over sin, disease, and demons.

Aimee Semple McPherson was a member of the Assemblies of God for only three years (1919-1922), but it was her great campaigns (before, during, and after these years) which placed innumerable "Council" churches on the map. Before "Sister Aimee" came, many of the assemblies were but small, struggling missions in city after city: Washington, D. C., Baltimore, Philadelphia, Rochester, Akron, Dayton, Canton, Tampa, Miami, Jacksonville, St. Louis, Chicago, Wichita, Tulsa, Denver, Dallas, San Diego, Los Angeles, San Francisco, Montreal, and Toronto. Everywhere Mrs.

McPherson preached, mammoth crowds were attracted and the attention of churches and ministers was drawn to the Pentecostal message.[21]

Aimee Semple McPherson was a dynamic and dramatic individualist, and it is doubtful that she could ever have been a permanent member of any organization except her own. It might have been mutually beneficial for her to remain in the Assemblies of God: her evangelistic ministry could have possibly tripled its growth, and, in turn, she would have benefited by the moderating influences of a conservative organization. Nevertheless, the splendid organization which she founded, The International Church of the Foursquare Gospel, has been wondrously blessed of the Lord, and is one of our staunchest allies.

Smith Wigglesworth, the "Apostle of Faith," came to America from England on repeated evangelistic tours during the twenties. No other person exerted more influence over the Assemblies of God with regard to faith for supernatural confirmation of the Word than this one-time illiterate English plumber. His little book *Ever-Increasing Faith* sold over one-hundred thousand copies. To be in one of his inspiring services, to sing with him, "Yes, filled with God," and to witness the miracle-working power of God was truly an unforgettable experience.

Ben Hardin was a national figure in evangelism in these days. His anointed preaching, wry humor, and extraordinary number of conversions and baptisms made him a highly popular evangelist. One businessman was so thrilled with Hardin's sermon "The Lost Axehead" that he offered him $1,000 to come to his city for just one night and preach it there. No hireling, Hardin declined. In one of his frequent Minneapolis campaigns a young boy was healed of an eye affliction. Appearing at school the next day without his glasses, the lad was commanded to go home and get them; his teacher would not listen to "any of this divine healing nonsense." When her pupil returned, she was astonished to

<hr>

[21]*Dr. Charles S. Price* and *Dr. Charles A. Shreve* were two of many prominent Pentecostal evangelists who came into Pentecost through the ministry of Mrs. McPherson. Their city-wide crusades, camp meetings, and conferences gave a great impetus to the Assemblies of God.

discover that, while he could not see at all with the glasses on, he could see perfectly with them off! This boy became an Assemblies of God pastor and Assistant Superintendent of the South Florida District, and national secretary of Stewardship and Benevolences and Home Missions—Curtis W. Ringness.

The diminutive Texan (can anything *small* come out of Texas?) *Raymond T. Richey* ran to the altar one night in 1911 to answer the invitation given by A. P. Collins. Throughout World War I and the Flu Epidemic which followed Richey labored unceasingly among the servicemen, many of them finding Christ on their deathbeds with their hands clasped in his hand. Weakened by his strenuous labors, he fell prey to tuberculosis, which put him on his back in a California hospital.

Elijah-like, Richey prayed that he might die. God graciously reminded him that he had been miraculously healed of an eye disease not long after his conversion, that his mother had been delivered from this same dreaded tuberculosis, and that the church back home was having special prayer for him at this very hour. Richey took his Bible and read Psalm 103:3: "Who forgiveth all thine iniquities; who healeth all thy diseases." Creeping slowly from his bed and staggering weakly back and forth across the room, with his Bible raised overhead, Richey murmured, "I praise you, Lord, I know that you are healing me." Each time he repeated these words his voice grew louder, until he was shouting at the top of his lungs. In that hour he was made "every whit whole"!

It was only normal to expect such a man to have an exceptional divine healing ministry. But he had to be thrust into it. In the fall of 1920, Richey was assisting Warren Collins in revival meetings. Acting as the advance agent, he made all the arrangements for the campaign in Hattiesburg, Mississippi, only to receive a telegram from Collins stating that he would be unable to come. Desperate, Richey wired for instructions. Back came the answer: "Preach yourself." The first night there were fifteen people present, and the second night not many more. The third night a

young woman with a crooked arm was healed. The fourth
night the auditorium was packed, and for three weeks souls
were saved and filled, and the sick were healed. Thus began the ministry of Raymond T. Richey, who confessed,
"I have not been called to preach, but I have been called
to put faith into action." God gave him a ministry which,
for miracles of healing and lasting results, was at least the
equal of any contemporary evangelist.

How shall we tell of the great campaigns of *Jack
Saunders*, the former British sailor and prize fighter;
Harvey McAlister, the delightful expositor of divine healing
truth; *C. S. Tubby*, the Canadian Christian Crusader? Or
of *William F. Kirkpatrick*, the former circus bandsman, who
even today insists, "I am not superannuated but super-
animated; I am not retired but refired"? Or of *John J.
Ashcroft*, the stirring evangelist whose son, J. Robert Ash-
croft, served as the Spirit-filled President of Central Bible
College and Evangel College? Or of *Adolph Petersen, S.
Guy Shields, Meyer Tan Ditter*, and of the ministry of *John
Bostrom* and his brothers *A. N.* and *William*.

But surely it would be criminal neglect if we failed to
mention the heroic wives of Pentecostal evangelists. Some
of these ladies were able to accompany their husbands, and
thus share in the revival blessings, and also share in the
unbelievable hardships of pioneer fields and in the uncom-
fortable adjustments of living constantly in the homes of
strangers. Other wives stayed with the children, enduring
perpetual loneliness and vainly attempting to run the household on the meager offerings which were sent home. No
wonder that these godly women turned to God! The story
of the discussion by two boys of the powerful prayer which
the mother of one had offered in the service certainly applied to these evangelists' wives:

"Boy, your Mom can sure pray," exclaimed the first
youngster.

"Yeah," replied his friend, "but she ought to be able to.
She spends a couple of hours every day up in the attic
practicing!"

And how can anyone amply chronicle the evangelistic

exploits of the once much-maligned "Women Preachers"? *Mabel Harrell,* whose "ministry was blessed to the healing of the sick" and whose son, J. Otis Harrell, served as the manager of the Gospel Publishing House? *Willa May Short* whose altar services were marked by the mighty presence of God? *Dr. Lilian Yeomans* whose ministry and whose book *Healing from Heaven* edified so many? *Hattie Hammond,* the girl evangelist, whose campaigns were already manifesting a depth and power that were to make her unique even among such contemporaries? *May Eleanor Frey,* the former newspaperwoman, whose dynamic preaching and writing evoked such widespread admiration that she was invited to preach the full gospel in the Mormon Tabernacle in Salt Lake City?

EVANGELISTIC FAMILIES

Three families were typical of the numerous families who, as a unit, spent years on the evangelistic field: The *Hirum Brookses,* the *James Cardiffs,* and the *W. J. Higginses.* Traveling over the highways and byways, playing their musical instruments, singing and preaching in tents, schoolhouses, homes, barns, brush arbors, and on street corners, these families went out by faith, usually not knowing exactly where they were going, but the record shows where they have been! First to declare the full-gospel ‚message in community after community, each family was successful in planting at least a score of assemblies. It was not easy, but as one pioneer preacher's wife put it, "It was so wonderful to see the people receive such glorious experiences that we forgot all about the hardships and constant insecurity." [22] Children of each family are in the ministry of the Assemblies of God today.

TEACHERS

It is frequently asserted that *all* that is needed by the Church is a Pentecostal effusion of the Spirit and fervent evangelism. However, the New Testament Church, which incorporated both of these vital elements, is abundant proof that something else is needed: a teaching ministry that will

---

[22] Mrs. Andrew F. Crouch, *op. cit.*

consolidate the gains of revivalism and evangelism. All pastors and evangelists did the work of a teacher at times, but there were a number of outstanding teachers who, while not as spectacular as some of their brethren, exercised a great stabilizing influence upon the Assemblies of God. [23]

Foremost among the teachers of this period was *Donald Gee,* of the British Assemblies of God. Gee's sound and spiritual sermons, articles, and books were invaluable to the young movement. Two of his compatriots, *Howard Carter* and *Harold Horton,* also "helped them much which had believed." The devotional writings of *Carrie Judd Montgomery, Elizabeth Sisson,* and *Beatrice Sims* lifted hearts closer to Christ. *David H. McDowell, W. B. McCafferty,* and *Charles E. Robinson* established thousands of souls in God. *A. G. Ward* could always be counted on for a profitable unfolding of the Book of Books. A doctrinal trio which had a great part in molding the conservative nature of the Assemblies of God was composed of *J. Narver Gortner, S. A. Jamieson,* and *P. C. Nelson.*

J. Narver Gortner was the son of a Methodist missionary who gave his life for the Lord in Liberia. Bishop William Taylor, the famed missionary, was an old and a dear friend of the Gortner family. Educated and ordained in Methodist ranks, "when every preacher was a revivalist," Gortner served a dual role as pastor of the Arroyo Grande, California, Methodist Church and as the chairman of a nearby M. E. camp meeting. At the close of his own camp in 1914, he decided to attend the Pentecostal camp meeting conducted by Carrie Judd Montgomery and Smith Wigglesworth among the redwoods in Cazadero, Calif.

The meetings were marvelous. I had never seen such mighty manifestations of the power of God. The glory of the Lord swept over the saints like the billows of the sea. It was "joy unspeakable and full of glory." And how the saints did sing! I watched the

<hr>

[23] *The Pentecostal Evangel* of July 7, 1923, carried this report by Pastor S. S. Johnson: "Brother J. C. Wilder is so quiet for a Pentecostal man that I felt a little uneasy about the Saturday night evangelistic service; but when I saw the large crowd listening attentively, and, when he was through preaching, the number with earnest faces coming forward for prayer, I was satisfied deep down in my soul. After all, it is lightning not thunder that kills. Truly, 'there are diversities of gifts.'"

seekers who were tarrying for the baptism in the Spirit. Everyone on the grounds knew I was a Methodist preacher. One day a person undertook to exhort me to seek the fullness. A woman stepped up and said, "Let him alone! God has his hand on this man, and God will see him through." And God did see me through. On the last day of the camp I went to my tent about twelve o'clock, committed my soul to God and slept like a child. I awoke as the day was breaking, and God reminded me of the words of Scripture, "And Jacob went on his way, and the angels of God met him." As I repeated these words aloud, the power of God fell on me and I began to speak in other tongues as the Spirit gave utterance.

The devil said, "It is a wonderful experience, of course, but you had better not say anything about it. Just live the experience and keep still." I opened the Word of God, and the first passage of Scripture my eyes rested upon was this, "I will declare what He hath done for my soul." Then the devil said, "It was just by chance your eyes lighted upon those words, and besides, if you tell these Pentecostal people here in Cazadero God has baptized you, you will have to testify in your church down at Arroyo Grande. They will think you have scandalized yourself and your church, and maybe they will put you out." I opened the Word of God again, and the first words I saw were, "Nevertheless, among the chief rulers many believed on Him, but because of the Pharisees they would not confess Him, lest they should be put out of the synagogue." I said, "Lord, I will tell the people God has baptized me with the Holy Ghost and fire," and at the first opportunity I did. [24]

At this camp Smith Wigglesworth laid his hands upon Gortner, and a serious spinal ailment was healed. In three or four days God gave this rather sickly preacher "a complete overhaul" from head to foot. Gortner remained with the church of his fathers for five more years, but severed his formal connection with Methodism in 1919, attended the General Council that year in Chicago, and gave this testimony:

I am a Pentecostal preacher tonight . . . I would not exchange what I have for all the wealth of the Goulds, the Vanderbilts, the Rockefellers and the Carnegies of earth. To be saved from sin and baptized with the Holy Ghost is worth more than ten thousand worlds like this.

The next five years were spent as a much-beloved pastor of the Cleveland, Ohio, assembly, followed by ten years of fruitful ministry in Oakland, California, and then by

---

[24] *Latter Rain Evangel*, November, 1919.

many years as an esteemed member of the faculty at Glad Tidings Bible Institute [25]

S. A. Jamieson, a Texan Presbyterian pastor, received a telegram to pray for rain. Having witnessed the "effectual, fervent prayer" of the Pentecostal saints in the little tabernacle down the street, he took his urgent request to them. "God of Elijah, hear our cry," they prayed, and God sent "an abundance of rain." Now intensely interested, Jamieson attended the 1912 Mary Woodworth Etter meeting in F. F. Bosworth's church in Dallas, where his rather detached objectivity became radiant subjectivity, when he was filled with the Spirit. Resigning his church, Jamieson became an associate pastor in the Dallas assembly. Though a scholarly man, he was filled with zeal to proclaim the full gospel to illiterate backwoodsmen; and though used to the comforts of life, and an older man, he cheerfully put up with the inconveniences of the hinterland. But his brethren insisted that his ministry should be broadened to include the established assemblies, and for years Jamieson ministered with great insight and power to many needy hearts across the land.

P. C. Nelson was a Baptist pastor in Detroit when he came into contact with the full gospel. Severely injured as a result of being struck by an automobile, Nelson was healed through the prayer of a Pentecostal woman. Her testimony concerning the baptism in the Spirit caused this college and seminary graduate to seek God.

I couldn't understand why one had to tarry. I thought that the Holy Spirit came at Pentecost. Why did I have to tarry? Then I found out why. I was full of things that had to come out, and there seemed to be no end to the things, like the things which a magician takes out of his clothes and hat. I had no room for anything else . . . I had to clean out to make room for the Holy Spirit. Maybe it would not be necessary for you to tarry so long, but it was surely necessary for me . . . I had seen people receive the Baptism in a few minutes after conversion, but I found out that I had to "tarry until." [26]

P. C. Nelson was "endued with power from on high,"

---
[25] *Ibid.*
[26] *Pentecostal Evangel,* January 16, 1926.

and became one of the strongest exponents of the Pentecostal message. He preached, wrote, and established a Bible school in Enid, Oklahoma, which afterward became the Southwestern Bible College. His excellent library he donated to this institution. Above all, Nelson exemplified the supernatural faith which he taught by his exceptional ministry in praying for the sick and for those seeking the infilling with the Spirit. His sage counsel at General Council sessions was also of great value.

The chief emphasis of these Pentecostal teachers was upon *scriptural balance.* "Don't go overboard in any direction ... keep in the middle of the road." A certain amount of latitude was permitted in regard to doctrines and practices held by the individual but it was recommended that those views which were not generally accepted should not be pushed until they divided an assembly.

For example, the difference of opinion in regard to footwashing as an ordinance. Many early Pentecostalists had practiced this rite, and real blessing had attended their ministry to one another in this humble fashion. Nor were the stock arguments against its position as an ordinance too convincing. Later, the brethren began to take a second look at this question. While not being too proud to participate in its observance, and with no desire to condemn those who sincerely practiced it in their services or to dictate to sovereign congregations, the great majority rejected footwashing as an ordinance for the following reasons:

1. The words Christ used when instituting the Lord's Supper, "as *oft* as ye," are missing from His words concerning footwashing in John 13.

2. There is no subsequent instance of footwashing recorded in the Scriptures, which indicates that the New Testament church did not practice it as an ordinance.

3. Paul's words in 1 Timothy 5:10, "if she have washed the saints' feet," are not in a context of a religious service but of household duties, and her guests would, in most cases, be "saints," for whom it sometimes takes more grace to perform menial tasks than for sinners.

The same conservatism was exhibited in the matter of

external holiness. A firm stand was taken against worldliness,
but it was generally recognized that holiness is primarily a
matter of the heart. Consequently, while worldly practices
were defined and denounced, no fetish was made of mere
externalism. Galatians 5:16 was an oft-quoted text: "Walk
in the Spirit, and ye shall not fulfill the lusts of the flesh."
In his Question and Answer column in *The Pentecostal
Evangel* (August 20, 1921) E. N. Bell advised:

> Where it is customary to wear a gold ring, and considered wrong
> for the wife not to wear it, let her wear it ... but don't let the
> Christian woman take advantage of the custom of wearing this
> simple wedding ring to deck out with loads of gaudy jewelry just for
> worldly show.

A resolution passed by the General Presbyters in later
years [27] expressed the desire for doctrinal balance which
characterized the twenties:

> Whereas, word has been brought to the General Presbyters that
> contention is arising in some sections by those who are strongly
> teaching that a person must have the baptism with the Holy Ghost,
> speaking with other tongues, in order to be ready for the Rapture,
> and whereas, it is the belief of this body that those who are born
> of the Spirit and walking in the light have the promise of being
> ready when Jesus comes, therefore be it resolved, that we dis-
> approve this extreme teaching which only tends to breed controversy
> instead of unity and fellowship.

Pentecostalists have had a tendency to ascribe too much
importance to the amount of emotionalism in the service
and to the size of the crowd. God is interested in both,
and we must be, too; but it is necessary to have the right
perspective. These wise words of the mighty Joseph Tunmore are typical of the admonitions given by many spiritual
men in the Assemblies of God:

> Getting crowds is not all that is needed. You can have crowds and
> still not have God's purpose accomplished. There are plenty of
> people having crowds, but the power of the Spirit is not manifest
> in their midst. Moving in God is what counts. He says, "I will
> instruct and teach thee in the way thou shalt go. I will guide thee
> with mine eye." So let us get to the place where we can find out
> God for ourselves and move in Him ... Moving independently of the

---

[27] 1946, General Presbyters' Notes.

Holy Ghost is something we all have to guard against continually ... Our spirits must sense thoroughly what is God and what is not God ... A person can start a meeting going like a great flywheel, and it will take God all the rest of the service to get it quiet. The people become wrought up into such a pitch that you cannot possibly get the mighty power of God in such a service [28]

The constant aim of the fellowship was to produce a balance between enthusiasm and conservatism; to exhibit a freedom that was not fanaticism, an informality that was not irreverence, a dignity that was not deadness, a purity that was not pharisaism. The degree to which this aim was achieved in the twenties, made the Assemblies of God enormously appealing, to thousands of Christians who were inclined toward the Pentecostal Movement.

---

[28] *Latter Rain Evangel,* November, 1916.

CHAPTER **11**

"PERSECUTION ARISETH"

Verily I say unto you, There is no man that hath left house, or brethren, or sisters, or father, or mother, or wife, or children, or lands, for my sake, and the gospel's, but he shall receive an hundredfold now in this time, houses, and brethren, and sisters, and mothers, and children, and lands, with persecutions; and in the world to come eternal life.[1]

The "hundredfold" expansion of the twenties was accompained by persistent and, at times, violent persecution. Early Pentecostalists "received the work in much affliction," but also, "with joy in the Holy Ghost." They learned to take the bitter with the sweet.

One form of persecution that caused much heartache among Pentecostal believers was ostracism from fellow Christians. Opposition from the world was expected, but it hurt when "those of like precious faith" passed resolutions like the following overwhelmingly adopted in a Chicago Fundamentalist Convention, reported in *The Pentecostal Evangel* (August 18, 1928) :

Whereas, The present wave of Modern Pentecostalism, often referred to as the "tongues movement," and the present wave of fanatical and unscriptural healing which is sweeping over the country today, has become a menace in many churches and a real injury to the sane testimony of Fundamental Christians, Be it Resolved, That this convention go on record as unreservedly opposed to Modern Pentecostalism, including the speaking with unknown tongues, and the fanatical healing known as general healing in the atonement, and the perpetuation of the miraculous sign-healing of

---

[1] Mark 10:29-30.

140

Jesus and His apostles, wherein they claim the only reason the Church cannot perform these miracles is because of unbelief."

Editor Frodsham commented:

Although the Fundamentalists have by this action disfellowshiped a great company of us who believe in all the fundamentals of the faith as much as they themselves do, we will, by the grace of God, continue to love and fellowship every child of God.... We Pentecostal people may be "without the camp," but we do not condemn those who do not see as we do. "Show me divine healing in the Scripture," said one defiantly to a saint whom the Lord graciously uses in praying the prayer of faith for the sick. "I cannot show it to you," said the worker, "I can only point out to you the scriptures on the subject; it will have to be the Holy Spirit who shows you the truth."

Donald Gee, writing in the May 18, 1929, *Pentecostal Evangel,* asked, "Why Is 'Pentecost' Opposed?" and listed as the most frequent causes, tradition, doctrinal disagreement, unbelief, fear, jealousy, and conviction. "Some of the most spiritual movements of past decades are among the fiercest opponents of 'Pentecost.' The last wave to break on the shore is, as it recedes, the chief opponent to the oncoming rush of the tide." Certainly, many "devout and honorable" men and women were stirred up to attack the oncoming rush of Pentecostalism.

In Yellville, Arkansas (what better place to start the story of persecution of Pentecost?), *John Davis,* a convert of the great Thayer, Missouri, Revival of 1907-9 (which produced twenty-six churches), was conducting a brush arbor meeting. Seven preachers notified him that they were coming to debate with him about the Pentecostal teaching. Davis was distressed, for, though a firm believer and preacher of the message, he did not consider himself able to defend it against these sharpshooters. He went to prayer, lying all night long before the rough altar (just a few years before he had spent many nights lying dead drunk in the road before a saloon). The next night, even before the meeting was formally opened, the Lord baptized twenty in the Spirit, and the slain of the Lord were many. It was evident to the preachers that the debate would not take place; a higher power had taken over, and Davis looked up just in time to see the last of the forensic seven slink away.

Occasionally, the "devout and honorable" were stirred up to more than vocal opposition. *Paul Jones,* a barber in Yellville, plied his trade to support his large family while preaching Pentecost (the only critics of his "tent making" he said, were men with small families and big churches). Jones tells of a revival in the White River country in which

a large number of unsaved church members got under conviction and were saved and filled with the Spirit, the Bible way . . . It was more than their old pastor could stand. You see, it was a brush arbor, and he would stand behind a tree. He sent me word that if any more of his members came to that altar, he would drag me out of there and beat me up, and he was big enough and mean enough to do it. I fasted and prayed all the next day. The people had heard of it, and they came from everywhere to see what would happen.

Well, that night God's message was burning me up, and I jumped upon that old, rude altar and preached it with all my heart. All three of the aisles were full of people coming to seek God, and soon the altar was full and others were kneeling in the front seats. I looked and saw that fighting preacher coming toward me, so I closed my eyes and whispered to Almighty God to take care of him. When I opened my eyes to see what God had done with him, he was lying prostrate in the sawdust. God had knocked him down, as He did Saul of Tarsus. To Him be all the honor, glory and praise![2]

Paul Jones was a real pioneer, barbering by day and riding horseback by night fourteen miles to his revival meetings. Oftentimes he had to walk the railroad bridge, since he couldn't afford the ferry. A merchant provided a goods box for a pulpit which provided a helmet for this warrior.

When we began to pull the cover off sin, and preach the gospel with old-time power, the devil and his gang got stirred up, and began to throw rocks from out in the dark—they loved darkness, for their deeds were evil. Well, I did not care for the rocks hitting my body, but since I already had a big scar on my head, I didn't want any more rocks hitting my head. That's why I turned the open side of the box toward me, so I could put my head inside it when I was praying. The devil was defeated. In fact, I found out that the harder the battle, in most cases, the greater the victory![3]

---

[2] Paul Jones, *My Life's Story,* pp. 6, 7.
[3] *Ibid.*

Jones was "down in the swampy bottoms of Arkansas," when he received word that a brush arbor had been built for him in Lawrence County about 200 miles away. He announced the close of the meeting, promising to return to erect a church. That night a group of men who had been his most violent opposers sent him word that they wanted to be baptized. This was apparently a genuine answer to prayer, for Jones had obeyed the command to "pray for them that despitefully use you." But just as God warned the Wise Men to return another way, so God warned Jones not to go to the White River to keep the baptismal rendezvous. He saw in a flash that their purpose was to drown him: this murderous plot was later exposed. God knoweth how to keep His own!

Frank Gray was one of the Pentecostal leaders who bore the brunt of physical persecution. His son, Harold F. Gray, writes:

It was in early 1918 that a wave of persecution was directed toward my father by some of the neighbors in the farming area where we lived, about 20 miles west of Spokane, Washington. The hatred in these men increased until one evening a group came to the house and forcibly removed him, took him out and literally "tarred and feathered" him. I was sleeping at the time he came home, but I heard noises downstairs, and I came and saw my mother scraping the tar from his body and bathing him.[4]

S. B. Drew [reported S. Clyde Bailey] was the first person I ever baptized. He became a great preacher and won many souls to the Lord. What persecutions he endured! I saw him after he had been beaten, tarred and feathered, and left for dead. God marvelously healed him, and he lived to preach the full gospel for over twenty-five years.[5]

Bailey also recalls a slightly less violent incident in Ripley County, Missouri:

In a revival meeting some boys emptied a whole box of cayenne pepper upon the rostrum. People shouting and rejoicing soon raised a cloud of pepper, and the congregation began to sneeze. I rebuked the sneezing, and every trace of it stopped suddenly. This brought a great calm over the people, and many believed. God got glory out of the incident. The devil always oversteps himself.[6]

[4] Letter to author, Sept. 1, 1959.
[5] Clyde Bailey, *op. cit.*
[6] *Ibid.*

Oscar Jones who received the Spirit's fullness in Seymour, Texas, in 1909, wrote in the _C. A. Herald_ (November, 1956) of his ministry in Oklahoma and Texas:

After giving their hearts to Christ, many men poured out their home-brew and liquor and destroyed their stills. Naturally, it made the devil mad that he was losing his crowd to the Stronger One, so he moved upon some of his still loyal subjects to persecute the servants of the Lord. While we conducted services in Jacksboro, Texas, rocks and rotten eggs were thrown at us, and a plot was made to blow up our house. Providentially, two little girls discovered the dynamite and warned us in time. Many people were healed in this town ... God worked miracles in spite of the opposition of Satan.

Walter J. Higgins, who with his family opened more than 25 churches, relates:

In April, 1912, after conducting a revival in a converted saloon in Canalou, Mo., in which a hundred received the Baptism, and more than that were saved, my wife and I moved to Morehead to begin pastoring a small group of people. Occasionally, I returned to Canalou to preach. After a service there one night, I had a strange burden to pray all night. My hostess came to me the next morning and asked why I had remained in the church all night. I could not answer, for I did not know why.

Shortly after, I went to the station to catch a train.... Having bought my ticket, I was approached by a stranger who asked me if my name was Higgins. When I replied in the affirmative, he asked me to step outside. At that moment another man stepped up and began to curse and to abuse me. Then he pounded my head with his fists, knocked me down, and stomped on my head and sides with his heel. Scarcely able to move, I climbed to my feet, throbbing with pain all over. "Have you had enough?" he asked foolishly. "Brother, why have you treated me this way?" I whimpered. In a moment a crowd of men had gathered, and when they recognized me, they wanted to kill my assailant on the spot. I pleaded with the men to do him no harm, explaining that God would repay ... I later learned that my attacker had been paid four dollars to beat me. Three days after this brutal attack, he was bumming his way out of town on a freight train when he slipped between the cars and his body was severed in two pieces. Having seen the accident, several men stated, "That is what a man gets for beating a preacher." I could clearly understand what the Apostle Paul meant when he mentioned beatings, etc.[7]

---

[7] _C. A. Herald,_ November, 1956.

Beating up the preacher seemed to be a favorite sport in other communities. *L. A. Sappington* recalls that in Oregon County, Missouri, where he had a circuit of thirteen small churches,

a rancher . . . hired ten men to break up the meeting and beat up the preacher. He asked a prominent stock buyer to oversee the attack. The night the assailants came to the meeting, the Lord mightily anointed me to preach. Before the men could start to wreck the brush arbor, the Lord convicted the stock buyer. With a heart-rending cry, he ran to the altar and repented of his sin. About sixty people were saved that night.

In this town we had received permission to use a church built for the use of all denominations. When the Lord had begun to bless, the church officials became angry and we were evicted. Later, we were given permission to conduct services again in the building. One of the officials fired four shots at me through a window with a ten-gauge shotgun. I was hit by shattered glass, but suffered no gunshot wounds. The official, a lifelong resident in the community, became frightened, sold his farm, and left the community less than a week later. Through these experiences, the Lord was at my side.[8]

Walter C. Long, with a group of workers from the South Cumberland, Maryland, Assembly, pitched a tent in Flintstone, Maryland, a distance of about ten miles to the East, in the spring of 1920. This was mountain country on the border between Maryland and Pennsylvania and the tent lot was called "The Devil's Half-Acre." Thirty-five were saved and twelve received the fullness of the Spirit. Two sons of a moonshiner were converted, and to add insult to injury, one-third of his wheat crop was destroyed by a storm. Blaming Long and his meetings for his misfortunes, he persuaded a gang of men to burn down the store building to which the services were shifted. The flames shooting into the mountain sky on April 20, 1921, signalled the start of two and a half years of guerrilla warfare.

Long was awakened about four o'clock one morning, a few weeks later, by the sound of someone at the door of his home. Thinking that it was a sick call, he hurriedly dressed and came to the door just in time to hear an object land at his feet, and to hear a car drive away. When

---

[8] *Ibid.*

he saw the object spluttering, he knew that it was a bomb. He picked it up, failed to extricate the fuse, so threw it into a field just before it exploded. A second bomb thrown from the car he was able to defuse with two stones. Running to his deacon's house down the road, Long saw another bomb under it, and he managed to toss it away just in time. Just then, a third bomb exploded under Long's own house, blowing out the windows and damaging the walls. The Flintstone Bomber meant business! A subsequent bomb knocked two small sons of a Pentecostal believer out of bed. The frightened father came running to Long, "What are we going to do? They're going to kill us yet!"

Clearly, this was no place for softies. Harold Moss, principal of the Beulah Heights Bible School, in New Jersey, once brought a group of students into this danger-filled area. Long warned him: "If you see me get excited, watch out! Otherwise, whatever happens is just routine." Nothing untoward occurred during the day or in the early part of the service, so Moss began to preach with the feeling that perhaps the danger had been exaggerated. Suddenly the night was shattered by an ear-splitting sound, the windows were shattered and the building was rocked by a terrific explosion. Moss turned as white as a sheet. Long looked at him calmly, "Preach on, my brother, you're still standing!"

Ten miles northeast of Flintstone lay Chaneysville, Pennsylvania, where the embattled Pentecostal believers sought to establish a second assembly. For three weeks there was no break. Eating no "pleasant bread," spending days in fasting and prayer, the little group fought against the powers of hell. One night, as Long stood up to preach, a strange heaviness fell on all the people. One by one, the workers went to sleep, and it was not because of the length of the sermon or the lateness of the hour. Long himself felt as though he was being choked.

Suddenly, Long threw both hands into the air, and cried, "In the name of Jesus, I rebuke this thing!"

At that instant, according to people outside the tent, a ball of fire came down from the sky and struck the tent.

Saints and sinners fell to the ground as though machine-gunned, both within and without the tent, even in the buggies. One frightened woman ran 100 yards to her home, fell across the doorway and was immediately filled with the Holy Ghost. The "slain of the Lord" were crying, shrieking, screaming for mercy. The few unaffected ones ran to those on the ground, lifting their heads and giving them water to drink. One big timberman strode down the aisle, "What's going on here?" he roared. At that moment the power of God hit him, and down he went like a huge tree. The service which lasted far into the night stirred the whole countryside.

Long was permitted to conduct afternoon services in a lovely church in Chaneysville, even though some of the members of the church were in violent opposition. Seventeen men signed an ultimatum, demanding that he discontinue his meetings there. As he approached the building one afternoon, six armed men barred his way.

"Long, you can't go into this church."

"Why, what evil have we done?"

"You're Pentecosters, and this is a .... church."

"Yes, but no one else is holding services here now. Are you all members of the church?" The leader, obviously drunk, nodded his assent.

Long saw a man draw a gun, and he quickly said, "Put that up. We don't want any trouble here. We are not going to force our way into your church. All I want to know is, would you rather have the bats and moles take over this place, or have the gospel preached here?" Their answer was a sullen mutter, "You're Pentecosters."

Waving his arm toward the church, Long cried, "Then let the bats and moles have it," and walked away.

This beautiful church, valued at more than $100,000, became the scene of drunken orgies by this crowd; not one service was ever conducted therein, and it served as a habitation of bats and moles until it was torn down in 1957.

The "Pentecosters" lived in a state of siege, in circum-

stances similar to those of the pilgrims who took their guns
to church in early America. To protect their families, the
men were forced to leave the place of worship and fight off
the ugly mobs that stormed against the doors. Returning,
they resumed their seeking of God, "lifting holy hands"
that were bruised and bloody, and if not "without wrath,"
at least "without doubting"! It must be remembered that
these men were mostly lumberjacks who took care of the
situation in the only way they knew. Considering the
situation, one can be tolerant about their adopting Old
Testament methods to defend the New Testament Gospel.

Two unsaved men, whose wives, mothers, and sisters
were members of the congregation, kept constant vigil in
the building that the "Pentecosters" were seeking to erect.
World War I veterans, these men slept in the unfinished
church for several months. One night a car drove up—
the Flintstone Bomber and his wrecking crew. "Sure would
make a pretty fire, wouldn't it?" growled a voice. Picking
the leader out in the dark, one of the guards had his gun
leveled at him, but his buddy whispered that he must hold
his fire until the intruders actually committed some crime.
The attackers heard the whisper and dived for cover under
a nearby bank, and opened fire. After a furious, hour-
long exchange, one of the defenders slipped quietly out of
the back of the building, outflanked the enemy, lined up
all five in his sights and let go with a blast of buckshot that
sent them all howling for home!

A truce prevailed for a time, and the building was finally
completed. Long journeyed to Martinsburg, West Virginia,
to conduct a revival campaign. He planned to return soon
to dedicate the edifice which the men had toiled so
agonizingly to erect, dragging the heavy timbers from
swamps up to the horses' bellies. The men, tired of fighting
and hoping that the truce was permanent, relaxed their
vigilance. On August 5, 1923, disaster struck. Ninety-two
sticks of dynamite were slipped under the new building and
the explosion scattered it all over the countryside!

It was four long years before the broken-hearted congregation succeeded in putting up another house of worship,

but this one stayed up. Meanwhile, the persecution continued unabated. Five men were wounded when twenty-three shots were fired into a temporary building. One believer, stopping for gas on the way home from church, discovered three sticks of dynamite wired to his battery. Providentially, the battery wasn't working, so he had used the magneto. "Brother," he exclaimed, "I was a lot nearer to heaven than I knew when I was driving down the road tonight singing and shouting!"

Informers were planted in the services. Buggies were burned, harnesses and even the horses cruelly slashed, automobile tires punctured and cut to ribbons. Wheels were loosened so that they would come off on the precipitous mountain roads. The law always seemed to arrive after the trouble was over.

Nevertheless, the undaunted soldiers of the Cross took the message to Green Ridge, Maryland, thus completing a triangle. Here they met not only the old Flintstone crowd but also the local toughs. All preachers but one, a Methodist, had been run out of the town in the past years. That parson had watched one horseman ride into the church, up the aisle and across the platform. Quietly following him outside, the preacher yanked him off his horse, and disposed of him with one punch, and knocked out two of his companions. He, for obvious reasons, was permitted to stay!

Long, a former heavyweight prize-fighter, was also able to defend himself. Hence, the opposition decided to import a huge fellow who had beaten the best men in Bucks County, Pennsylvania. Half-drunk and mean, he came raging into the tent one evening just after the altar call. Three rows of praying people knelt between him and Long. The two stood eyeing one another. Suddenly, the intruder gave a cry of pain, and, clutching his thigh, limped out into the dark. After the service, a constable accused Long of stabbing the fellow.[9] Long disclaimed any knowledge of such a thing, supposing that the Lord had dealt with the man. Still, the

---

[9] The law always seemed to side with the persecutors. When a telegram was received at the 1959 General Council conveying greetings of the President of the United States to the delegates, a speaker from the floor observed: "Today we receive a telegram from the President, while it seems only yesterday that we received an order from the sheriff to get out of town!"

next night, as a tiny, frail woman with a sailor hat came into the tent, his suspicions were aroused.

"Sister, did you see that fellow that came in last night at the close?"

"Yes, that big bully spat tobacco juice on my shoes, and I jabbed him with a pin."

Somewhat shaken, Long asked to see the pin.

"Oh just this little old pin." From her handbag the dainty little sister drew a murderous looking six-inch long, blue-steel hat pin.

"Bless God," she cried, "I ran it right through him!" [10]

Two events contributed to a halt in this violent persecution. A deacon whose patience had reached an end, went to the general store and asked to buy all the 30-30 shells in the store. "Why?" asked the owner rather suspiciously. "Well, we Pentecostal people have been taking and taking—about ten blows for every one that we felt that we just had to give back. Now I'm tired of taking. All we want to do is to worship God and we are going to protect that freedom in the only way that is open to us." When word got around the hills that the church folks had forty dollars worth of 30-30 shells, it became a little more difficult to assemble a crowd of attackers.

The second event was the assistance of a converted son of the Pentecostal Enemy Number One, the Flintstone Bomber. Assured that the church people would not physically hurt his father, the boy led Long and the men of the congregation to the straw pile where the church-wrecking and house-destroying bombs were stored. It proved to be identical with the bomb which Long had preserved and, when presented in court in Cumberland, Maryland,

---

[10] Remember, we are not advocating—only reporting! It does remind us of the tale concerning a Methodist preacher who was forced to use unorthodox means to create respect for the house of God. A husky youth was disturbing the service, and after being warned twice, he bolted for the door with the parson right after him. Up the hollow they ran, with the clergyman's coattails flying in the air. Concerning the disturber, the man of God handled him somewhat roughly and marched him back toward the church. "Why don't you practise what you preach about love and grace?" whimpered the young fellow accusingly. "Boy," growled the preacher between clenched teeth, "you had better thank God I do practice what I preach, because if it were not for that love and grace, you would sure be a mess right now!"

at the trial of the Bomber, it resulted in a $3,000 fine. This hurt him badly enough for him to call off the war.

Paul's warning that "all that live godly in Christ Jesus shall suffer persecution" was literally fulfilled in these pioneers. Their faith, courage, determination showed that they were willing to "hazard their lives" for the Lord Jesus. The early days were marked by fierce persecution, but assemblies were established and the opposition was finally overcome. Well might the twentieth-century persecutors have accepted the wise counsel given to their counterparts in the first century by Gamaliel:

Refrain from these men, and let them alone; for if this counsel or this work be of men, it will come to naught: but if it be of God, ye cannot overthrow it; lest haply ye be found even to fight against God.[11]

---

[11] Acts 5:38, 39.

CHAPTER **12**

RIPENING YEARS

"You can't keep a good man down" is an axiom with a definite application to E. N. Bell. After his recantation of his temporary and partial acceptance of Oneness teaching, Bell took a small pastorate in Galena, Kansas, where, under normal circumstances, he would have faded from view behind a cloud of suspicion and doubt. Bell, however, possessed such qualities of leadership that in 1918 he was restored to his old post of Editor of the *Evangel;* in 1919 he was elected to the office of General Secretary, and in 1920 the brethren voted him back into the Chairmanship, a post he occupied until his death in 1923. The hand of God was in this restoration, for Bell, as no other man, championed the autonomy of the local assembly as the true foundation of Assemblies of God polity. At the same time, Bell insisted on the holding of church property by the assembly through trustees rather than by any individual and likewise on the clause in the deed stating that the property reverts to the Assemblies of God, if the local assembly is ever dissolved.

John W. Welch, who had served as Chairman from 1915 to 1920 and who had changed positions with Bell in 1920, was re-elected Chairman upon Bell's death in 1923. Two other able men came into office at this time: *D. H. McDowell,* as Assistant Chairman, and *J. R. Evans,* as Secretary. McDowell remained in this office until 1929 and greatly aided the expansion of the Assemblies of God by his wise counsel at headquarters and by his excellent field ministry. Evans served as Secretary for twelve years.

He was noted for his phenomenal memory and his ability to recall the names and addresses of many ministers on the roll. Evans also exercised a steadying influence during these years, helping to acquaint two General officers with their new role. (The titles of the presiding officers until 1927 were Chairman and Secretary. The titles were changed in the 1927 Council to General Superintendent and General Secretary.)

The General Council of 1925 [1] returned to the state of its birth, Arkansas. The Eureka Springs Council was a momentous one. Prior to this Council, the business had been guided by the resolutions adopted during the sessions; in fact, these resolutions had been the only specific guide for all headquarter's operations. Therefore, Welch and Flower drew up a pamphlet for presentation to the Eureka Springs Council: "Interpretation of the Constitutional Agreements and Essential Resolutions Recommended by the Executive Presbytery, 1925."

Brother Welch explained that the Executive Presbytery was not trying to put something over on the Council. He had been too long in the Council work to even think of such a thing. The pamphlet was merely suggestive and had been submitted for the prayerful consideration of those attending the Council. [2]

Although the executive brethren proceeded with extreme caution, disclaiming any desire for denominational bondage, they ran into a storm of protest. This gathering of individualists felt that there was more than a simple constitution involved; they imagined they were faced with the loss of local sovereignty and the building of a huge ecclesiastical machine. And there were, indeed, a few elements in the pamphlet that would have made the most open-minded soul suspicious. For example, the Chairman and the Secretary were to be called "President" and "Vice President" and the General Council was termed "the governing body"!

Despite appeals for love, unity, and confidence in the brethren who had submitted the pamphlet, the discussion ran strongly against its adoption.

---

[1] It was decided in 1921 that the General Council should meet biennially.
[2] *Pentecostal Evangel*, October 10, 1925.

On Monday morning the authors of the new interpretation brought forward a resolution tabling all the contents of the pamphlet until the Council met in 1927. Immediately, an amendment was presented that this matter be tabled indefinitely. When the amendment was put to the vote, the brethren were unanimous in voting for it.[3]

Actually, with the exception of a few objectionable features, the pamphlet was only an attempt to put into systematic and permanent form the resolutions that the body itself had adopted from Council to Council, and the freedoms that some feared would be lost were fully guaranteed therein. Between the 1925 and 1927 Councils, J. R. Flower and Harold Moss prepared a constitution for the Eastern District which embodied all of the essential resolutions. J. Narver Gortner made some constructive changes in this District Council constitution, edited it to fit the General Council, and submitted it to the 1927 Council, where it was adopted without a dissenting vote!

The earlier proponents of the constitution, however, fell by the wayside in the Eureka Springs Council. Welch and Flower paid the price of being before their time, both being voted out of office, and neither being brought back to Springfield until some years later; Welch in 1931, as business manager of Central Bible Institute, and Flower in 1935, as General Secretary (though Flower was elected in 1931 as a nonresident Assistant General Superintendent, which office he held until 1937.)

W. T. Gaston was elected Chairman on the fifth ballot of the divided 1925 Council. This was home territory for the popular Gaston whose ministry had been largely in the Southwest. As a young man in Arkansas, he was known as the "walking preacher," having hiked hundreds of miles over "the worst roads that God ever let afflict the earth." As a pastor in Springfield, Missouri, and Tulsa, Oklahoma, Gaston had demonstrated administrative ability, and he was universally acknowledged to be one of the most forceful and anointed preachers in the entire Pente-

---

[3] *Ibid.*

costal Movement, as attested by this report of the 1920 Russellville, Arkansas, Camp Meeting:

> God used A. P. Collins and W. T. Gaston in a most blessed way, and the power of God fell like rain the last few days of the camp ... The last night, while Brother Gaston was preaching, the power of God began to come down, till hundreds were moved, and a great rush was made by hungry hearts to touch God. The altar service was a blaze of glory, and a dozen or more souls prayed through in the old time way ... The crowds were large at all the services. Newspaper men estimated the attendance at three thousand the last night.[4]

Gaston had a fast-growing organization over which to preside. Twenty-one District Councils had now been formed, and in those days the presence of the Chairman at the District Council sessions was considered almost a necessity. In addition, the administrative duties had increased in direct proportion to the growth of the fellowship. The management of the Gospel Publishing House was enough in itself to occupy the attention of one man. Sunday school literature poured forth from this Pentecostal center in ever-mounting thousands of pieces each year; books by Pentecostal writers were eagerly bought by the people and Pentecostal songbooks by the churches; more than a million tracts were being printed annually. In 1926 J. R. Evans, the Secretary, was given the herculean task of managing the Gospel Publishing House, but it soon became apparent that a full-time man was needed. *J. Z. Kamerer,* who had been in the printing department since 1919, was chosen for this position, and this appointment proved to be one of the wisest choices ever made. A man of God whose steady Christian life blessed all and an excellent businessman, Kamerer deserves much credit for the tremendous growth in the volume of business.

Two other wise decisions were made at this time by the Executive Presbyters. *Charles E. Robinson,* the Arkansas lawyer-turned-preacher, was named Associate Editor of *The Pentecostal Evangel,* a position he was to fill with distinction for twenty-one years. His excellent book *Praying to Change Things* and his "Around the World" stories for

---

children revealed the versatility of his pen; and his Men's Bible Class at Central Assembly was a joy to attend. The second decision was the authorization of *Stanley H. Frodsham* to write the story of the Pentecostal outpouring. *With Signs Following*, which concentrated on the spiritual aspect of this Movement, proved to be an immensely popular book.

In Watertown, New York, in the spring of 1926, a distinct impression came to a young pastor, while in prayer, that a change was coming soon in his ministry. The next mail contained a letter from J. R. Evans, inviting him to assist in the business management of the Gospel Publishing House. Banking experience in England and Canada had qualified this pastor for the post, but his experience as a missionary to Argentina pointed toward a position more directly related to foreign missions. Nevertheless, he told his wife, "I have a quiet feeling that this offer is of God."

Shortly after his arrival in Springfield, this young man saw his dream begin to unfold. W. T. Gaston asked him to assist William Faux, who was the current Missionary Secretary-Treasurer. The following year upon the resignation of Faux, he was asked to assume this chief missions post. If ever an office and a man were made for each other, such was true of this foreign missions secretariat and *Noel Perkin*. For thirty-three years Perkin brought total dedication to this ministry: he lived, ate, drank, talked, dreamed, and sacrificed for missions.[5] Perkin's spiritual vision, his vast grasp of the problems of the field, his business acumen, his compassion and understanding have spearheaded the phenomenal growth of Assemblies of God missions around the globe. Is it any wonder that the respect and affection for Noel Perkin within the fellowship is not one whit less than for any other man?

---

[5] A missionary once noted that the earpiece on Perkin's glasses was patched together in a "do-it-yourself" fashion, and thinking this strange for an executive, he asked for an explanation from the secretary. She replied that Perkin so often received urgent and heart-rending appeals from the field for which there were no funds, that he himself would try to meet the need personally; hence, the neglected glasses

The twenties also witnessed the birth of the youth organization within the Assemblies of God. And it started in California! *Wesley R. Steelberg,* the youthful pastor of the Sacramento assembly, and *Carl Hatch,* the Los Angeles musician and preacher, formed separate youth groups; Steelberg, the "Pentecostal Ambassadors of Christ" and Hatch, the "Christ's Ambassadors." The latter name was eventually chosen [6] for the entire youth work of the Assemblies of God. It was the far-seeing vision of both men that sparked the formation of youth groups all over the nation. Some ultraconservatives were voicing their doubts concerning this move, but Kansas Superintendent, *Fred Vogler,* speaking at a tri-state rally in Springfield, Missouri, January 1, 1927, said, "I consider the nation-wide formation of Pentecostal youth societies the greatest forward move we have had in Pentecost since the founding of the General Council." The 1929 General Council recognized the validity of both views by passing a resolution expressing approval of these youth societies and permitting them to elect officers and to appoint committees, but also admonishing them to work closely with their churches and pastors. That the Christ's Ambassadors have fully justified Vogler's prophecy and averted any inherent dangers from becoming reality is evidence of the approval of God upon this step.

The year 1925 will live long in the memories of the ladies of the fellowship, for it was in this year that *Etta Calhoun* began, in Houston, Texas, the first Women's Missionary Council. Resolutions had been broached at several General and District Councils in this direction, but it had been feared that such gatherings might degenerate into mere social clubs. Nonetheless, this brave daughter of Texas had courageously inaugurated this means of fulfilling the desire of Pentecostal women to do ˜their part in promoting the kingdom of God. It was a small beginning, and it did not catch fire for many years, but the Women's Missionary Council was to be a tremendous

---

[6] Inadvertently preventing this youth group from being confused with the P.A.O.C., "Pentecostal Assemblies of Canada"!

boon to missionaries at home and abroad, to Bible schools, and to local assemblies.

The election of *Ernest S. Williams* as General Superintendent at the 1929 General Council signalled a new era for the Assemblies of God. The days of experimentation were over. Crises had been met, and God had caused the young movement to triumph. Now He had chosen a man of wisdom and integrity from his pastorate in Philadelphia to lead this burgeoning Pentecostal organization. Youthful and yet a veteran of Azusa days, Williams was a link between the past and the present. For twenty years under God he was to guide the destiny of this revival fellowship.

In reflecting on the foundational years of the Assemblies of God, let it be stated again that the stories recorded here of early Pentecostal heroes of the faith could be repeated with only slight variation to describe the labors of countless other hundreds of men and women of God. And may we never forget the price by these "sowers of the Word" to insure an abundant harvest. [7]

> Whene'er you ripe fields behold
> Waving to God their sheaves of gold,
> Be sure some corn of wheat has died,
> Some saintly soul been crucified.
> Someone has suffered, wept and prayed
> And fought Hell's legions undismayed.

Some made the supreme sacrifice. Carved upon a simple Nicaraguan tombstone, erected to the memory of Clarence Radley, an Assemblies of God missionary who died in 1926, are the poignant words: *"Sembró la Palabra Divina a costo de su vida."*—"He sowed the Divine Word at the cost of his life."

---

[7] For a complete history of the Assemblies of God, see *Anointed to Serve*, by William W. Menzies (Springfield, Mo: Gospel Publishing House, 1971).

ARTICLE V.
STATEMENT OF FUNDAMENTAL TRUTHS

The Bible is our all-sufficient rule for faith and practice. This Statement of Fundamental Truths is intended simply as a basis of fellowship among us (i.e., that we all speak the same thing, 1 Cor. 1:10; Acts 2:42). The phraseology employed in this Statement is not inspired or contended for, but the truth set forth is held to be essential to a Full-Gospel ministry. No claim is made that it contains all Biblical truth, only that it covers our need as to these fundamental doctrines.

1. The Scriptures Inspired

The Scriptures, both the Old and New Testaments, are verbally inspired of God and are the revelation of God to man, the infallible, authoritative rule of faith and conduct (2 Tim. 3:15-17; 1 Thess. 2:13; 2 Peter 1:21).

2. The One True God

The one true God has revealed himself as the eternally self-existent "I AM," the Creator of heaven and earth and the Redeemer of mankind. He has further revealed himself as embodying the principles of relationship and association as Father, Son, and Holy Ghost (Deut. 6:4; Isaiah 43:10,11; Matt. 28:19; Luke 3:22).

THE ADORABLE GODHEAD

(a) Terms Defined
The terms "Trinity" and "persons," as related to the Godhead, while not found in the Scriptures, are words in harmony with Scripture, whereby we may convey to others our immediate understanding of the doctrine of Christ respecting the Being of God, as distinguished from "gods many and lords many." We therefore may speak with propriety of the Lord our God, who is One Lord, as a trinity or as one Being of three persons, and still be absolutely scriptural (examples, Matt. 28:19; 2 Cor. 13:14; John 14:16,17).

(b) Distinction and Relationship in the Godhead
Christ taught a distinction of Persons in the Godhead which He expressed in specific terms of relationship, as Father, Son, and Holy Ghost, but that this distinction and relationship, as to its mode is inscrutable and incomprehensible, because unexplained. Luke 1:35; 1 Cor. 1:24; Matt. 11:25-27; 28:19; 2 Cor. 13:14; 1 John 1:3,4.

(c) Unity of the One Being of Father, Son, and Holy Ghost
Accordingly, therefore, there is that in the Son which constitutes Him the Son and not the Father; and there is that in the Holy Ghost which constitutes Him the Holy Ghost and not either the Father or the Son. Wherefore the Father is the Begetter, the Son is the Begotten; and the Holy Ghost is the One proceeding from the Father and the Son. Therefore, because these three persons in the Godhead are in a state of unity, there is but one Lord God Almighty and His name one. John 1:18; 15:26; 17:11,21; Zech. 14:9.

(d) Identity and Cooperation in the Godhead
The Father, the Son, and the Holy Ghost are never identical as to Person; nor confused as to relation; nor divided in respect to the Godhead; nor opposed as to cooperation. The Son is in the Father and the Father is in the Son as to relationship. The Son is with the Father and the Father is with the Son, as to fellowship. The Father is not from the Son, but the Son is from the Father, as to authority. The Holy Ghost is from the Father and the Son proceeding, as to nature, relationship, cooperation and authority. Hence neither Person in the Godhead either exists or works separately or independently of the others. John 5:17-30,32,37; John 8:17,18.

(e) The Title, Lord Jesus Christ
The appellation, "Lord Jesus Christ," is a proper name. It is never applied, in the New Testament, either to the Father or to the Holy Ghost. It therefore belongs exclusively to the Son of God. Rom. 1:1-3,7; 2 John 3.

(f) The Lord Jesus Christ, God with us

The Lord Jesus Christ, as to His divine and eternal nature, is the proper and only Begotten of the Father, but as to His human nature, He is the proper Son of Man. He is, therefore, acknowledged to be both God and man; who because He is God and man, is "Immanuel," God with us. Matt. 1:23; 1 John 4:2,10,14; Rev. 1:13,17.

(g) The Title, Son of God

Since the name "Immanuel" embraces both God and man in the one Person, our Lord Jesus Christ, it follows that the title, Son of God, describes His proper deity, and the title Son of Man, His proper humanity. Therefore, the title, Son of God, belongs to the **order of eternity**, and the title, Son of Man to the **order of time**. Matt. 1:21-23; 2 John 3; 1 John 3:8; Heb. 7:3; 1:1-13.

(h) Transgression of the Doctrine of Christ

Wherefore, it is a transgression of the Doctrine of Christ to say that Jesus Christ derived the title, Son of God, solely from the fact of the incarnation, or because of His relation to the economy of redemption. Therefore, to deny that the Father is a real and eternal Father, and that the Son is a real and eternal Son, is a denial of the distinction and relationship in the Being of God; a denial of the Father and the Son; and a displacement of the truth that Jesus Christ is come in the flesh. 2 John 9; John 1:1,2,14,18,29,49; 1 John 2:22,23; 4:1-5; Heb. 12:2.

(i) Exaltation of Jesus Christ as Lord

The Son of God, our Lord Jesus Christ, having by himself purged our sins, sat down on the right hand of the Majesty on high; angels and principalities and powers having been made subject unto Him. And having been made both Lord and Christ, He sent the Holy Ghost that we, in the name of Jesus, might bow our knees and confess that Jesus Christ is Lord to the glory of God the Father until the end, when the Son shall become subject to the Father that God may be all in all. Heb. 1:3; 1 Peter 3:22; Acts 2:32-36; Rom. 14:11; 1 Cor. 15:24-28.

(j) Equal Honor to the Father and to the Son

Wherefore, since the Father has delivered all judgment unto the Son, it is not only the **express duty** of all in heaven and on earth to bow the knee, but it is an **unspeakable** joy in the Holy Ghost to ascribe unto the Son all the attributes of Deity, and to give Him all the honor and the glory contained in all the names and titles of the Godhead (except those which express relationship. See paragraphs b, c, and d), and thus honor the Son even as we honor the Father. John 5:22,23; 1 Peter 1:8; Rev. 5:6-14; Phil. 2:8,9; Rev. 7:9,10; 4:8-11.

3. The Deity of the Lord Jesus Christ

The Lord Jesus Christ is the eternal Son of God. The Scriptures declare:

(a) His virgin birth (Matthew 1:23; Luke 1:31,35).

(b) His sinless life (Hebrews 7:26; 1 Peter 2:22).

(c) His miracles (Acts 2:22; 10:38).

(d) His substitutionary work on the cross (1 Cor. 15:3; 2 Cor. 5:21).

(e) His bodily resurrection from the dead (Matthew 28:6; Luke 24:39; 1 Cor. 15:4).

(f) His exaltation to the right hand of God (Acts 1:9,11; 2:33; Philippians 2:9-11; Hebrews 1-3).

4. The Fall of Man

Man was created good and upright; for God said, "Let us make man in our image, after our likeness." However, man by voluntary transgression fell and thereby incurred not only physical death but also spiritual death, which is separation from God (Genesis 1:26,27; 2:17; 3:6; Romans 5:12-19).

5. The Salvation of Man

Man's only hope of redemption is through the shed blood of Jesus Christ the Son of God.

(a) Conditions to Salvation

Salvation is received through repentance toward God and faith toward the Lord Jesus Christ. By the washing of regeneration and renewing of the Holy Ghost, being justified by grace through faith, man becomes an heir of God according to the hope of eternal life (Luke 24:47; John 3:3; Romans 10:13-15; Ephesians 2:8; Titus 2:11; 3:5-7).

(b) The Evidences of Salvation

The inward evidence of salvation is the direct witness of the Spirit (Romans 8:16). The outward evidence to all men is a life of righteousness and true holiness (Eph. 4:24; Titus 2:12).

6. The Ordinances of the Church

(a) Baptism in Water

The ordinance of baptism by immersion is commanded in the Scriptures. All who repent and believe on Christ as Saviour and Lord are to be baptized. Thus they declare to the world that they have died with Christ and that they also have been raised with Him to walk in newness of life. (Matthew 28:19; Mark 16:16; Acts 10:47,48; Romans 6:4).

(b) Holy Communion

The Lord's Supper, consisting of the elements—bread and the fruit of the vine—is the symbol expressing our sharing the divine nature of our Lord Jesus Christ (2 Peter 1:4); a memorial of His suffering and death (1 Cor. 11:26); and a prophecy of His second coming (1 Cor. 11:26); and is enjoined on all believers "till He come!"

7. The Baptism in the Holy Ghost

All believers are entitled to and should ardently expect and earnestly seek the promise of the Father, the baptism in the Holy Ghost and fire, according to the command of our Lord Jesus Christ. This was the normal experience of all in the early Christian Church. With it comes the enduement of power for life and service, the bestowment of the gifts and their uses in the work of the ministry (Luke 24:49; Acts 1:4,8; 1 Cor. 12:1-31). This experience is distinct from and subsequent to the experience of the new birth (Acts 8:12-17; 10:44-46; 11: 14-16; 15:7-9). With the baptism in the Holy Ghost come such experiences as an overflowing fullness of the Spirit (John 7:37-39; Acts 4:8), a deepened reverence for God (Acts 2:43; Heb. 12:28), an intensified consecration to God and dedication to His work (Acts 2:42), and a more active love for Christ, for His Word, and for the lost (Mark 16:20).

8. The Evidence of the Baptism in the Holy Ghost

The baptism of believers in the Holy Ghost is witnessed by the initial physical sign of speaking with other tongues as the Spirit of God gives them utterance (Acts 2:4). The speaking in tongues in this instance is the same in essence as the gift of tongues (1 Cor. 12:4-10,28), but different in purpose and use.

9. Sanctification

Sanctification is an act of separation from that which is evil, and of dedication unto God (Rom. 12:1,2; 1 Thess. 5:23; Heb. 13:12). The Scriptures teach a life of "holiness without which no man shall see the Lord" (Heb. 12:14). By the power of the Holy Ghost we are able to obey the command: "Be ye holy, for I am holy" (1 Peter 1:15,16).

161

Sanctification is realized in the believer by recognizing his identification with Christ in His death and resurrection, and by faith reckoning daily upon the fact of that union, and by offering every faculty continually to the dominion of the Holy Spirit (Rom. 6:1-11,13; 8:1,2,13; Gal. 2:20; Phil. 2:12,13; 1 Peter 1:5).

10. The Church and Its Mission

The Church is the Body of Christ, the habitation of God through the Spirit, with divine appointments for the fulfillment of her great commission. Each believer, born of the Spirit, is an integral part of the General Assembly and Church of the Firstborn, which are written in heaven (Ephesians 1:22,23; 2:22; Hebrews 12:23).

Since God's purpose concerning man is to seek and to save that which is lost, to be worshiped by man, and to build a body of believers in the image of His Son, the priority reason-for-being of the Assemblies of God as part of the Church is:

a. To be an agency of God for evangelizing the world (Acts 1:8; Matthew 28:19,20; Mark 16:15,16).
b. To be a corporate body in which man may worship God (1 Corinthians 12:13).
c. To be a channel of God's purpose to build a body of saints being perfected in the image of His Son (Ephesians 4:11-16; 1 Corinthians 12:28; 1 Corinthians 14:12).

The Assemblies of God exists expressly to give continuing emphasis to this reason-for-being in the New Testament apostolic pattern by teaching and encouraging believers to be baptized in the Holy Spirit. This experience:

a. Enables them to evangelize in the power of the Spirit with accompanying supernatural signs (Mark 16:15-20; Acts 4:29-31; Hebrews 2:3,4).
b. Adds a necessary dimension to worshipful relationship with God (1 Corinthians 2:10-16; 1 Corinthians 12,13, and 14).
c. Enables them to respond to the full working of the Holy Spirit in expression of fruit and gifts and ministries as in New Testament times for the edifying of the body of Christ (Galatians 5:22-26; 1 Corinthians 14:12; Ephesians 4:11,12; 1 Corinthians 12:28; Colossians 1:29).

11. The Ministry

A divinely called and scripturally ordained ministry has been provided by our Lord for the threefold purpose of leading the Church in: (1) Evangelization of the world (Mark 16:15-20), (2) Worship of God (John 4:23,24), (3) Building a body of saints being perfected in the image of His Son (Ephesians 4:11-16).

12. Divine Healing

Divine healing is an integral part of the gospel. Deliverance from sickness is provided for in the atonement, and is the privilege of all believers (Isaiah 53:4,5; Matt. 8:16,17; James 5:14-16).

13. The Blessed Hope

The resurrection of those who have fallen asleep in Christ and their translation together with those who are alive and remain unto the coming of the Lord is the imminent and blessed hope of the church (1 Thess. 4:16,17; Romans 8:23; **Titus** 2:13; 1 Cor. 15:51,52).

14. The Millennial Reign of Christ

The second coming of Christ includes the rapture of the saints, which is our blessed hope, followed by the visible return of Christ with His saints to reign on the earth for one thousand years (Zech. 14:15; Matt. 24:27,30; Revelation 1:7; 19:11-14; 20:1-6). This millennial reign will bring the salvation of national Israel (Ezekiel 37:21,22; Zephaniah 3:19,20; Romans 11:26,27) and the establishment of universal peace (Isaiah 11: 6-9; Psalm 72:3-8; Micah 4:3,4).

15. The Final Judgment

There will be a final judgment in which the wicked dead will be raised and judged according to their works. Whosoever is not found written in the Book of Life, together with the devil and his angels, the beast and the false prophet, will be consigned to everlasting punishment in the lake which burneth with fire and brimstone, which is the second death (Matt. 25: 46; Mark 9:43-48; Revelation 19:20; 20:11-15; 21:8).

16 The New Heavens and the New Earth

"We, according to His promise, look for new heavens and a new earth wherein dwelleth righteousness" (2 Peter 3:13; Revelation 21,22).

After, Assemblies of God Benevolence Department.

Apostolic Faith, Azusa Street Mission, Los Angeles, Calif.

Apostolic Faith, Baxter Springs, Kansas.

Apostolic Faith, Portland, Oregon.

Awrey, Daniel, *Telling the Lord's Secrets.*

Bailey, S. Clyde, *Pioneer Marvels of Faith.*

Ball, H. C. and Alice Luce, *Glimpses of Our Latin American Work,* Gospel Publishing House, Springfield, Mo.

Barratt, Thomas B., *In the Days of the Latter Rain, When the Fire Fell,* Elim Publishing Co., London, England.

Bartleman, Frank, *How Pentecost Came to Los Angeles,* 1925.

Berg, Vernon E., *Pentecost Every Day.*

Bibliotheca Sacra, Dallas Theological Seminary, Dallas, Texas.

Bresson, B. L., *History of the Michigan District of the Assemblies of God.*

Brumback, Carl, *What Meaneth This?* Gospel Publishing House, Springfield, Mo., 1947. *God in Three Persons,* Pathway Press, Cleveland, Tenn., 1959.

Burnett, C. C. and Carl Conner, *Early History of the Assemblies of God,* Gospel Publishing House, Springfield, Mo.

Campbell, Joseph, *The Pentecostal Holiness Church,* Pentecostal Holiness Publishing House, Franklin Springs, Ga., 1961.

Christ's Ambassadors Herald, Springfield, Mo.

Christian Evangel, Plainfield, Ind., and Springfield, Mo.

Christianity Today, Washington, D.C.

Christian Life, Chicago, Ill.

Clark, Elmer T., *The Small Sects in America,* Pierce & Smith, New York and Nashville, 1949.

Conn, Charles, *Like a Mighty Army,* 1955, *Where the Saints Have Trod,* 1959, Church of God Publishing House, Cleveland, Tenn.

Crayne, Richard, *Holy Ghost Power from on High,* 1957; *Early 20th Century Pentecost,* 1960, Morristown, Tenn.

Dalton, Robert C., *Tongues Like As of Fire,* Gospel Publishing House, Springfield, Mo., 1945.

D' Aubigné, Thomas, *History of the Great Reformation.*

District Chronicle, North California and Nevada District of the Assemblies of God.

Etter, Mary Woodworth, *Marvels and Miracles; Signs and Wonders,* Indianapolis, Ind., 1922.

Ewart, Frank, *The Phenomenon of Pentecost,* Pentecostal Publishing House, St. Louis, Mo., 1947.

Flower, Alice R., *My Mother's Healing; Grandmother Flower's Story.*

Flower, J. Roswell, *The Origin and Development of the Assemblies of God.*

164

BIBLIOGRAPHY

Frodsham, Stanley H., *With Signs Following*, 1946; *Apostle of Faith*, 1946; Gospel Publishing House, Springfield, Mo.

Full Gospel Men's Voice, Santa Ana, Calif.

Garrison, Winfred E., *The March of Faith*, Harper & Bros., New York, 1933.

Gee, Donald, *Upon All Flesh*; *The Glory of the Assemblies of God*; *The Pentecostal Movement*, Elim Publishing Co., London England.

Glover, Robert Hall, *The Progress of World-Wide Missions*, Harper & Bros., New York, 1924.

Gordon, Ernest, *Leaven of the Sadducees*, Moody Press, Chicago, 1926.

Goss, Howard and Ethel, *The Winds of God*, Comet Press, New York, 1958.

Graves, F. A., *So He Made It Again*.

Harrison, Irvine J., *A History of the Assemblies of God*, Th.D. thesis, Berkeley Baptist Divinity School, Berkeley, Calif., 1954.

Hardman, Marlin C., *The Retreat from Orthodoxy, in Theological Schools*, M.R.E. thesis Columbia Bible College, Columbia, S.C., 1958.

Harvester, The, Kansas District of the Assemblies of God, 1956.

Hastie, Eugene N., *History of the West Central District*.

Johnson, Elva, *Mission U.S.A.*, Gospel Publishing House, Springfield, Mo., 1957.

Jones, Paul, *My Life Story*, Harrison, Arkansas.

Kendrick, Klaude, *The Promise Fulfilled*, Gospel Publishing House, Springfield, Mo., 1961.

King, Joseph H. and Blanche L., *Yet Speaketh*, Pentecostal Holiness Publishing House, Franklin Springs, Ga.

Kulbeck, Gloria, *What God Hath Wrought*, Pentecostal Assemblies of Canada, Toronto, 1959.

Lang, G. H., *The Earlier Years of the Modern Tongues Movement*, Wimborne, Dorset, England.

Lawrence, B. F., *The Apostolic Faith Restored*, 1916.

Latter Rain Evangel.

Lindblad, Frank, *The Spirit Which Is from God*, Gospel Publishing House, Springfield, Mo., 1923.

McGowman, Mrs. C. M., *Another Echo from Azusa*.

McPherson, Aimee Semple, *The Story of My Life*; *This Is That*, Los Angeles, 1923.

Mayer, F. E., *The Religious Bodies of America*, Concordia Publishing House, St. Louis, Mo., 1956.

Minutes of the General Council of the Assemblies of God, 1914-1959.

Montgomery, Carrie Judd, *Triumphs of Faith*.

Munhall, L. W., *Breakers Ahead, Methodism Adrift!* Chas. C. Cook Co., New York, 1913.

Ozarks Mountaineer.

Nelson, P. C., *Bible Doctrines*, Gospel Publishing House, Springfield, Mo., 1940.

Parham, Sarah, *Life of Charles H. Parham*, Joplin, Mo.

Paulk, Earl P., *The Pentecostal Baptism; Sanctification; The Godhead and Its Members*, Cleveland, Tenn.

Paulk, Earl P., *Your Pentecostal Neighbor*, Pathway Press, Cleveland, Tenn., 1958.

Pearlman, Irene, *Myer Pearlman and His Friends*.

Pearlman, Myer, *Knowing the Doctrines of the Bible*, Gospel Publishing House, Springfield, Mo., 1937.

Pentecost.

Pentecostal Evangel, The.

Powell, Wilbur J., *The Christian Faith*.

Riggs, Ralph M., *The Spirit Himself*, Gospel Publishing House, Springfield, Mo., 1949.

Simmons, E. L., *The History of the Church of God*.

Sizelove, Rachel, *The Sparkling Fountain*.

Stalker, James F., *The Life of St. Paul*, Fleming H. Revell Company, New York.

Stegall, Carroll, Jr. and Harwood, Carl C., *The Modern Tongues and Healing Movement*, Western Bible Institute, Denver, Colo.

Thompson, A. E., *Life of A. B. Simpson*, Christian Publications, Harrisburg, Pa.

Tomlinson, A. J., *The Wonderful History of the Latter Rain*.

Tomlinson, Homer, *Diary of A. J. Tomlinson*, New York, 1949, Vols. I, II, III.

Tozer, A. W., *Wingspread*, Christian Publications, Inc., Harrisburg, Pa., 1943.

Trooster Comforter.

Weekly Evangel.

Williams, E. S., *Systematic Theology*, Vols. I, II, III, Gospel Publishing House, Springfield, Mo., 1953.

Winehouse, Irwin, *The Assemblies of God*, Vantage Press, New York, 1959.

INDEX

Evangel College, 92, 132
Evangelists, 129, 133
Evangelistic families, 133
Evangelists' wives, 132
Evans, J. R., 152, 153, 155
Evans, William I., 81, 89
Ewart, Frank, 42, 58

Fanaticism, 138, 139
False doctrine, 41, 138
Faux, William, 156
Fellowship, 13
Findlay, Ohio, 18, 37, 38
Florida, 101
Flower, Alice R., 48
Flower, J. Roswell, 17, 22, 23, 27,
  28, 40, 42, 43, 45, 47, 48, 49, 51,
  52, 61, 129, 153, 154
Floyd, Lee, 36
Fockler, Cyrus, 21, 28
Follette, John Wright, 79, 80, 85
Footwashing, 137
Foster, E. R., 127
Frank, Fred, 106, 124
Fraser, Andrew, 39
Frey, Mary Eleanor, 133
Frodsham, Stanley Howard, 54, 74,
  156

Garrett, C. C., 100
Garvin, W. F., 126
Gaston, W. T., 5, 16, 20, 70, 71, 72,
  73, 126, 155, 156
Gee, Donald, 134, 141
General chairman, 14, 15, 17, 20, 22,
  27, 38, 39, 51, 152, 153, 154
General superintendents, 20, 21, 36,
  94, 101
Gibeah Bible Institute, 78
Gifts, Spiritual, 66, 95, 134
Glad Tidings Bible Institute, 83, 84
Glad Tidings Tabernacle, 92
Glad Tidings Temple, 83
Goben, John, 5
Gortner, J. Narver, 84, 134, 135, 154
Gospel Publishing House, 88, 155,
  156
Goss, Howard, 4, 15, 24, 28, 47, 52,
  53, 58
Gotcher, T. J., 125
Graves, Fred A., 87
Gray, Frank, 128, 143
Greisen, V. G., 104

Haggard, Bright, 4
Hall, L. C., 47, 67
Hammond, Hattie, 95, 133
Hanson, C. M., 106
Hardin, Ben, 97, 105, 130
Harrell, J. Otis, 133

Harrell, Mabel, 133
Harris, Thoro, 4
Hatch, Carl, 157
Haywood, G. T., 4, 43, 47, 51, 58
Healing, divine, 20, 73, 94, 103, 104,
  105, 130, 131, 132, 133, 135, 136,
  143
Heavenly anthem, 80, 81
Hewson, Cmdr. Thos., 93
Highway Tabernacle, 94, 95
Hoar, Henry 104
Holy Spirit, 26, 44, 45, 52, 76, 77,
  78, 80, 82, 87, 96, 123, 139, 140
Holloway, D. P., 102
Horton, Harold, 134
Hot Springs, Ark., 5, 6, 7, 12, 15,
  27, 30, 32, 34, 36, 38, 43, 50, 56,
  67

Indiana, 43, 102-104
Indigenous, 67, 68
Intercession, 20, 23
Jamieson, S. A., 21, 54, 85, 134, 136
Jeffrey, Ralph, 95, 96
Jesus Christ, 2, 4, 8, 20, 25, 26, 29,
  33, 41-48, 52, 53, 56-59, 77, 83,
  87, 89, 96, 99, 102, 123, 125, 137,
  138, 141, 144, 146, 151
Jewelry, 138
Johnson, H. G., 124
Jones, Oscar, 144
Jones, Paul, 142, 143
Jones, T. J., 84

Kamerer, J. Z., 79, 155
Kansas, 63, 104, 105
Keener, Otis, 126
Kellner, John, 78
Kennemer, W. H., 126
Kentucky, 103
Kerr, D. W., 28, 44, 54, 55, 70, 72,
  73, 84, 86
Keyes, Leland, 84
Kirkpatrick, William, 132
Kline, J. R., 104
Knox, John, 28
Kolenda, John, 104
Kortkamp, A. W., 104

Lake, John G., 20
Lake Geneva Camp, 106
Lantz, Joseph, 125
Lasater, C. A., 5
Latter Rain Evangel, 5, 9, 69
Lawrence, B. F., 5, 21, 47
Lawson, K. H., 104
Levy, Mark, 58
Lewis, Gayle, 79, 104
Lindquist, Frank, 97, 105

168

Sinclair, John, 28
Sisson, Elizabeth, 134
Sizelove, Rachel, 64
Slye, John F., 95
Small, Frank, 49, 50
Smith, Charles, 47
Smuland, Mildred, 124
Smuland, Roy, 125
South Dakota, 105
Spanish-American work, 127, 128
Springfield, Mo., 61-65, 86-90, 96, 99
Steelberg, Wesley P., 94, 157
Steil, Harry J., 82
Stone Church, 38
St. Louis, Mo., 40, 42, 44, 45, 47, 50, 54, 61, 70
Swift, Allan, 81

Tan Ditter, Meyer, 132
Tanner, E. L., 102, 126
Taylor, Emma, 101
Teachers, 133, 134
Texas, 101, 144
Thayer, Mo., 141
Tongues, 26, 66-75, 98, 135, 138, 140
Trygg, Charles, 124
Trygg, Elmer, 124
Tunmore, Joseph, 71, 138
Turnbull, Louis, 129

Van Der Merwe, Stephen, 126
Van Gilder, Clara, 124
Van Loon, Harry, 47

Van Meter, Flem, 78, 103
Van Meter, James, 63
Vibbert brothers, 104
Voight, A. G., 101
Vogler, Fred, 16, 63, 78, 104, 157

Waggoner, George, 103
Waggoner, Harry, 103
Waggoner, John, 103
Walthall, W. Jethro, 70, 125
Ward, A. G., 99
Webb, Bert, 106, 123, 124
Webb, J. L., 101
Weekly Evangel, 43, 52, 54, 76
Welch, John W., 4, 5, 15-17, 20, 28, 51, 52, 53, 54, 56, 58, 152, 153, 154
Wesley, Charles and John, 100
What Meaneth This? 71
Wickman, Adeline, 124
Wigglesworth, Smith, 130
Wilder, J. C., 134
Wiles, H. C., 88
Williams, Ernest S., 83, 94, 95, 158
Williams, Mayme, 101
Wilson, A. A., 104
Winsett, R. E., 5
Wisconsin, 105, 123, 124
Women's Missionary Council, 125
Women preachers, 133
Word and Witness, 5, 6, 7, 14, 18, 27, 36, 44, 45

Yeomans, Lilian, 133
Youth, 16, 157

170